Past-into-Present Series

ESPIONAGE

Graeme Kent

B T BATSFORD LTD London

First published 1974
© Graeme Kent 1974

Typeset, printed and bound by
REDWOOD BURN LIMITED
Trowbridge & Esher
B. T. Batsford Ltd, 4 Fitzhardinge Street, London W1A 0AH
ISBN 0 7134 2806 6

Acknowledgments

The Author and Publisher would like to thank the following for the illustrations appearing in this book: The BBC for fig. 47; J. Anthony Chubb for fig. 6; Consolidated News Pictures for fig. 64; Sir Simonds D'Ewes for fig. 13; IAEA for fig. 50; The Keystone Press Agency for figs 37, 48, 49, 51, 52, 53, 54, 55, 56, 57, 58, 59, 60, 61, 62, 63; The Landersmuseum Trier for fig. 1; The Mansell Collection for figs 2, 3, 7, 8, 10, 11, 12, 15, 18, 19, 20, 22, 25, 26, 28, 29, 30, 31, 32, 33, 34, 35, 38, 39, 40, 41, 42, 43; The National Gallery for fig. 17; The National Portrait Gallery for fig. 9; Paul Popper Ltd for fig. 44; The Radio Times Hulton Picture Library for fig. 45; The Victoria and Albert Museum for fig. 16.

Contents

The Illustrations

1 The First Spies

Espionage, the art of spying, consists of obtaining secret information or of working secretly to harm an enemy. Spying is an ancient profession and secret agents have played an important part in human conflicts through the ages.

Over five thousand years ago the Egyptians had an efficient secret service. Their priests used paid informers to keep them in touch with what the ordinary people were saying and doing. In war, too, the Egyptians used ingenious methods of espionage. In about 3600 BC one of their leaders, Thute, was laying siege to a port that defended stubbornly and refused to surrender. He put two hundred of his men in flour sacks and smuggled them into the city in the hold of a neutral vessel. Once they were safely in the harbour the soldiers emerged from their flour bags and put the city to the sword.

Spies of the Old Testament
The first mention of spies in the Bible occurs when Moses is leading the children of Israel in their search for the promised land. God told Moses to send out spies into the land of Canaan. Moses at once selected some men to carry out this mission. He ordered them to make their way up into the mountains:

> And see the land, what it is; and the people that dwelleth
> therein, whether they be strong or weak, few or many.

Twelve spies were sent out on this mission and they returned carrying grapes and other fruit to show that the land was fertile. They also reported that the men of the district looked strong and that their cities were well fortified.

Two of the spies, Caleb and Joshua, were convinced that the Israelites could defeat the men of Canaan. They begged the others to invade the land that lay before them. But the ten remaining spies disagreed. They assured the assembled crowd that the men of Canaan were as big as giants and that the Israelites would be swallowed up if they attempted to raid the other country.

The Israelites were discouraged and believed the ten spies. They refused to attack Canaan. At this the Lord was very angry. He had intended the children of Israel to live in the land of Canaan, a land 'flowing with milk and honey'. But because they would not believe in his power to protect them he would now condemn them to forty years of wandering in the wilderness; all except Caleb and Joshua, the two spies who had wanted to invade Canaan. Because of their faith and courage God would allow them both to live in the land of milk and honey while the other Israelites were condemned to roam the desert.

1 This merchant vessel is transporting barrels of wine up a river. Such apparently innocent expeditions were often a cover for espionage. From earliest times merchants opened up new routes in their search for trade. Their knowledge was eagerly used by generals wishing to invade unknown territory. Sometimes during hostilities merchants continued to trade between opposing nations and were occasionally pressed into service or bribed to report on fortifications and troop movements

The twelve spies sent out by Moses were examples of one sort of agent: the man sent out to seek as much information as he could. Another type of spy is encountered in the Old Testament when the Israelites are coming to the end of their wanderings: the traitor who betrays his or her own people.

Moses had died and a warrior called Joshua was leading the Israelites. They were wandering across hostile territory and Joshua wanted to attack and capture the town of Jericho. Accordingly he sent two spies secretly into the town to gather information.

The spies spent the night with a woman of the town called Rahab. The king of Jericho heard that there were spies in the town and sent guards to search for them. Rahab hid the two spies and they escaped detection. When the soldiers had gone Rahab told the spies that she knew the Israelites were going to conquer

Jericho and that she would help them if they promised that she and her relatives would be spared.

The spies knew that they would probably be caught if they did not agree and so they made the promise. Keeping to her part of the bargain Rahab lowered them over the wall of the city to freedom. In return the spies gave her a scarlet cord. They told Rahab to gather all her family together in the house and to display the scarlet cord outside the house. The cord would be a sign that she had helped the Israelites, and no one in the house would be harmed. The woman did as she was told. When the Israelites finally stormed and took Jericho, killing many of its inhabitants, Rahab and her family were spared.

A third type of spy, the agent 'planted' to obtain information, is also portrayed in the Old Testament. This was Delilah, whom the Philistines used to trap Samson. Samson was a strong and mighty warrior and the Philistines, the enemies of Israel, tried very hard to subdue him, but in vain.

At last their opportunity came when Samson fell in love with a woman named Delilah, who lived in the valley of Sorek. The Philistines approached Delilah secretly and told her that if only she could find out the secret of Samson's great strength and if she could let them know how they might take him prisoner, they would give her eleven hundred pieces of silver.

Delilah accepted the bribe and agreed to act as an agent for the Philistines. She kept her part of the bargain well. She persuaded Samson to reveal that the secret of his enormous strength lay in his long hair, which had never been cut.

While Samson slept, Delilah called in a man who silently cut the strong man's hair. The Philistines seized Samson and as his strength had left him he could offer no resistance. He became a prisoner. Later his hair grew again and with it his strength returned. He was able to bring down the temple, killing himself and many of his enemies.

Legends

A sign that espionage was becoming well established as a part of warfare was that stories about spies and spying became incorporated into the legends of a number of early civilisations.

One of the most famous of these stories was the tale of the wooden horse of Troy. The Greek states had been laying siege to the city of Troy for ten years without succeeding in entering the city. One of the Greek leaders, Ulysses, ordered his men to build an enormous wooden horse. The horse was to be hollow, allowing room inside for a number of soldiers to be concealed.

So the Greeks built a huge horse. They told the Trojans that the horse was an offering to the goddess Athena. The Greeks then embarked their troops on their ships and sailed away. Inside the horse, however, a number of Greek soldiers had been hidden.

Slowly the Trojans emerged from behind the walls of their city in order to inspect the wooden horse left behind on the empty plain. One of their priests,

Laocoön, warned the Trojans to beware of the cunning Greeks, even if they had withdrawn. The priest threw a spear against the side of the wooden horse. It made a hollow sound.

The Trojans were about to destroy the horse when a Greek prisoner called Sinon managed to persuade them that they would offend the goddess Athena if they ruined her gift. As he spoke two serpents rose from the sea and devoured Laocoön and his two sons. This action convinced the Trojans that Sinon was right and that the goddess was furious with them. They broke down part of the city wall and dragged the wooden horse into Troy.

That night, while the Trojans were celebrating, Sinon crept over to the horse and opened a concealed door in its side. The Greek soldiers hurried out and threw open the gates of the city. The rest of the Greek force had returned silently and were waiting outside the walls. The Greeks rushed into Troy, killed many of the defenders and burned the city to the ground.

Another early legend involving the successful use of espionage involved a ruler called Histiaeus who died about five hundred years before the birth of Christ. At one time Histiaeus was a prisoner of the Persians. He desperately wanted to send an important secret message to his friends. The legend says that Histiaeus shaved the head of one of his slaves, tattooed the message on the shaven skull and when the man's hair had grown again he sent him safely through the Persians' lines. All that Histiaeus's friends had to do was to shave the head of the slave again in order to read the message.

The growth of espionage

With the passing of the centuries the use of espionage developed. Countries began to send ambassadors to one another. Their duties were supposed to include clearing up misunderstandings between nations and helping to develop trade. In reality an important function of an ambassador was to gather as much information as possible about the country he was living in and send it home to his masters. The Persians and the Chinese were particularly adept at this form of espionage.

Military leaders also needed accurate information about their enemies and potential enemies, and were eager to employ spies in order to obtain this information. One such general was Julius Caesar, commander of the Roman forces sweeping across Europe who, in 55 BC, set out to invade the unknown island of Britain.

First Caesar set to work to acquire information about the island. He ordered one of his officers, Publius Crassus, to collect as much information as he could from traders who had visited Britain. Publius Crassus also sailed to the south-west of Britain where there were tin mines. The people of that part of the island were accustomed to the arrival of strangers in search of tin, and Caesar hoped that they would talk freely to his spy.

Unfortunately Publius Crassus could discover little of value about Britain.

Caesar therefore decided to use another agent and to send this one right into Britain. He chose a leader of the tribe called the Atrebates. This man's name was Commius and he lived in Gaul. Julius Caesar had been fighting the men of Gaul but Commius had been loyal to the Romans and Caesar had made him a chief.

Commius was delighted to be chosen. He set sail for Britain accompanied by thirty mounted men. He had no intention of slipping unnoticed into the country. Commius reckoned that if he went with a show of force the Britons would be cowed and leave him alone, giving him an opportunity to spy out the land. Commius was wrong. Almost as soon as he and his men landed on the coast of Kent they were seized by the local inhabitants and imprisoned.

This meant that Caesar still knew little of the land he wanted to invade. Impatiently he sent for Gaius Volusenus, a tough and trusted military tribune. He ordered the officer to find a good landing place on the coast of Britain and not to come back until he had discovered one. Volusenus proved a good agent. Within three days he had found a suitable beach, ignoring the attempts of the Britons to

2 When the troops of Julius Caesar invaded the shores of England they met with spirited resistance from local tribes. Caesar had done his best to gather as much information as possible about England and the English, but his spies had met with little success. His leading agent, Commius, was over-confident and was captured and imprisoned before he could send any reports back to the Romans waiting in Gaul

3 Thrilling stories of spies and spying were as popular in the ninth century as they are today. Some of them were just as inaccurate! A popular legend was that Alfred, King of Wessex, dressed up as a minstrel and entered the camp of his Danish enemies as a spy, entertaining the Danes while he listened to their plans. The story appears to have had little or no basis in fact. Alfred was a most successful leader, however; he built a powerful fleet and established a network of forts

lure him ashore and capture him, and had reported back to Caesar.

Using the information provided by Volusenus, Caesar invaded Britain. The Britons defended their shores stubbornly and heavy storms drove the Romans' supply ships back to Gaul. However, Caesar managed to inflict one fairly decisive defeat on his foes. The Britons sued for peace and returned Commius and his men. Thankfully Caesar returned to Gaul.

The following year the Romans returned to Britain in greater strength. Again Caesar made use of espionage in his plans, persuading a tribe called the Trinovantes to join him in fighting the other tribes.

In AD 43 another Roman force landed in Britain and this time the Romans were to remain for over three hundred years. They were to be succeeded by waves of other invaders including Jutes, Angles and Saxons. All these newcomers first sent solitary ships ahead of the main body to spy out the land.

By the ninth century AD the Saxon King of Wessex, Alfred, was fighting desperately to protect his kingdom against the raiding Vikings. Alfred was perhaps the greatest Saxon king and he made use of a rudimentary intelligence service in order to obtain information about fresh Viking landings on the coast of Britain.

There is even a legend that Alfred dressed as a minstrel and made his way into the camp of his enemies, singing to them and at the same time sizing up their strength. However this story has never been confirmed, although the fact that ballad-makers were willing to portray their king as a spy shows how important secret agents were considered.

Further Reading——
Hortley and Pringle, *The Story of the Scriptures* (Schofield and Sims).
Burland, *Ancient Egypt* (Hulton).
Genest, *Myths of Ancient Greece and Rome* (Burke).
Chandon, *Stories from the Aeneid* (Burke).
Miliken, *The Roman People* (Harrap).
Coolidge, *Caesar's Gallic War* (Bodley Head).
Green, *Myths of the Norsemen* (Bodley Head).
Quennell, *Everyday Life in Anglo-Saxon, Viking and Norman Times* (Batsford).

2　Spies in the Middle Ages

Patriotism was not usually a highly-regarded virtue in the Middle Ages. Ordinary men did not often regard themselves as owing allegiance to their country but rather as having a duty to their own particular area or to an individual lord. This meant that while it was dangerous, it was not considered disgraceful to become a spy. If a man had information of value to dispose of he would look round for someone likely to buy it. So although there were plenty of individual spies, there were few organised espionage networks.

William the Conqueror

In Britain, Harold, the descendant of the original Viking invaders, was menaced in 1066 by William, Duke of Normandy, who claimed the throne of England. William built up an impressive force and prepared to take the throne from Harold.

While William was waiting for a favourable wind to take his ships across the Channel, English spies were at work in his camp. At least one agent was apprehended and brought before the duke. A contemporary account states that William was most contemptuous. The English king should be in no doubt about the duke's intention to invade his kingdom: 'Harold has no need to waste gold in buying the services of your kind', he told the spy.

According to the same account, the spy was promptly dispatched back to Harold to tell him that assuredly William would soon be following. Harold was too busy to pay much attention to the warning. While he had been waiting for William to strike in the south, Harold Hardrada of Norway had invaded Yorkshire in the north.

At once Harold marched north and defeated the invaders at the Battle of Stamford Bridge. But while he was in the process of killing Hardrada and slaughtering his force, William had crossed the channel and was waiting at Hastings in Sussex. Wearily Harold turned and began a forced march back to the south.

At his base near Hastings William was desperately in need of information. His agents and scouts could provide him with little. Then the Norman experienced a stroke of good fortune. He was aided by someone who, without meaning to do so, provided the Normans with invaluable information.

The inadvertent agent was Robert fitz Wimarc, who had originally come from Britanny but was now living in England. Wimarc had no desire to see the country of his adoption occupied by Normans. He therefore sent word to William that Harold had recently defeated the Norwegians and was now marching down to drive the Normans into the sea. He advised Duke William to withdraw while he still had the chance.

The advice was well meant and by giving it Wimarc had hoped to avoid bloodshed. However, the news of Harold's position and intentions was just what William had been waiting for. In his innocence Wimarc had provided him with more information than a dozen spies could have done. Secure in the knowledge that Harold was advancing, William was able to deploy his forces to fight the Battle of Senlac at Hastings. Harold was killed and his army defeated.

William became the ruler of England. He did not reign over a settled country. There were uprisings in Exeter, York and Durham, invasions from Denmark and Norway. William repulsed them all with great cruelty. He placed his own retainers in places of power and authority all over the country.

In a land ruled by hated foreigners William needed constant news of what was going on in his realm. This was provided to a great extent by his half-brother, Bishop Odo. Odo established a comprehensive intelligence service among his priests. He would not give an important living to a man unless he was sure that the priest would keep him fully informed of all that went on in his area. In time these priests formed an efficient intelligence service. They were the only men of education who mingled regularly with the ordinary people. They were in a special and privileged position to be of service to the Normans.

4 King Edward the Confessor is seen here giving advice to Earl Harold of Wessex. Shortly afterwards Harold set off for France. There he fell into the hands of Duke William of Normandy. William forced Harold to swear that he would give up his right to the throne of England in favour of William. When Edward the Confessor died Harold broke his word, which he said had been forced from him, and took the crown. William invaded England, defeated Harold at the Battle of Hastings in 1066 and became King William I of England, better known as William the Conqueror

England became a country torn by dissension. Those Norman barons to whom the king had given land vied with one another to see who could become the most powerful. It was an age in which information of any kind was eagerly snapped up and paid for. Communications were poor, and prominent among the purveyors of information were the wandering minstrels who moved from castle to castle, singing and telling stories for their keep. Merchants who sailed up and down the coast of the country kept their eyes and ears open and were perfectly willing in most cases to act as paid informers and part-time agents.

By playing his barons off against each other William ensured that none of them became too powerful and that he was informed by a jealous rival if one man looked like becoming richer or stronger than his fellows. Bishop Odo himself was betrayed in an act of rebellion and was imprisoned for the remainder of his life.

The rewards of espionage

The various monarchs who succeeded William in the Middle Ages realised that it was useful to have a steady supply of information, but few of them did anything concrete about building up an intelligence service. They relied on travellers and vagrants to provide them with news of what was going on in their kingdom. Spies were not a glamorous breed.

In the reign of Edward I, however, the first high-ranking spy in English history is recorded. This was Sir Thomas Turberville, one of the monarch's courtiers. In a war with France which began in 1293, Turberville was taken prisoner. While he was a prisoner he agreed to become a spy for the French king, Philip IV. The French arranged for their prisoner to 'escape', and Turberville returned to England.

Presumably the knight was well paid to betray his country because he set to work with a will. One of his tasks was to encourage the Welsh and the Scots to attack England, but he also submitted reports to the French on what was happening in court circles. One of these reports was intercepted by the king's censors who examined messages leaving the country. From the contents of the report it was obvious that Sir Thomas Turberville was a French spy. He was arrested, tortured until he confessed, and then executed. The fact that spying was still far from an art is revealed by the clumsy methods used by Turberville in order to communicate with the French.

Although English monarchs were always glad to have spies from other powers arrested and disposed of, their main concern was with the possibility of plots within the kingdom to topple them from the throne. Edward I, for example, expelled the Jews from his kingdom and was extremely suspicious of his own barons and even of the clergymen. Monarchs in other countries were equally suspicious of the Church, which had its agents scattered throughout Europe.

Kings who followed Edward I maintained his suspicious attitude and trusted few people. Edward III, who had come to the throne in 1327, while still a child, grew up in an atmosphere of hostility and intrigue. Some of his noblemen wanted

5 This fourteenth-century pope, seen here with his cardinals, probably controlled an extensive espionage service—like every other church leader in the Middle Ages. Priests in every country would keep the pope informed of what was going on. Some highly-placed courtiers considered their duty to the church was more important than allegiance to their country. Whichever pope was in power, he knew what was going on in all the courts of Europe

to overthrow him and give the crown to Philip of Valois. Edward was aware of this and he built up a small counter-espionage service. He paid a salary to the spies who worked for him, instead of paying them by results as had previously been the case. It was the duty of these men to smell out any plots against the king and to report such attempts at once.

Edward III seemed to possess a talent for intrigue, or else as a shrewd man he realised the necessity for remaining well-informed, because he also began to develop a rudimentary espionage service overseas. He maintained a secret agent, Count Niccolino del Fiesco, at the papal court in Avignon. His spy kept him in touch with what the Pope was doing and informed him about the intrigues and negotiations going on between the Church and other monarchs.

Following the lead given them by Edward III, other English kings maintained small intelligence services instead of relying on haphazard reports. These secret service organisations were the property of the kings themselves and were not part of any national defence plans.

The men who belonged to these espionage organisations varied in background.

6 Homeless vagabonds wandered all over Europe, owing allegiance to no country and serving all men. During their travels they sometimes stumbled across news of some importance, and this they were always willing to sell to the highest bidder

7 Richard Whittington, three times Lord Mayor of London, seen here with his cat which has been made famous in legend and pantomime. In reality Whittington was a shrewd and intelligent merchant who travelled extensively and was not above selling information. He was one of the first really wealthy spies in England, and lent money to three successive English kings: Richard II, Henry IV, and Henry V

Some of them were thieves and rogues, others were soldiers of fortune. A number of them were people with influential connections. Merchants who travelled a great deal continued to be used; one of these was the almost legendary Dick Whittington, later Lord Mayor of London, who served Henry V. These espionage organisations, comprising a nucleus of full-time agents and a larger number of part-time spies, did not always confine their activities to counter-espionage and putting down potential revolts. Sometimes they engaged in direct action.

One daring raid was ordered by Richard III. His throne was being threatened by Henry Tudor, who later became Henry VII. Henry was gathering an army in Brittany when a group of Richard's agents made their way over to Brittany with instructions to abduct Henry and bring him back by force to England. Fortunately for Henry, the plot was given away and his followers were able to foil the attempt.

8   A drastic but often effective means of obtaining information from a suspect was by torture!
In this dungeon a prisoner is about to be interrogated. A clerk is ready to take down his confession.
If it is not forthcoming quickly enough, a variety of implements are ready to be pressed into
service. Under the intense pain brought about by the rack, the thumbscrew and the hook, a man
would soon be ready to admit anything and give away anyone

Espionage under the Tudors

When Henry Tudor defeated Richard III at the Battle of Bosworth Field and became Henry VII, like most of his predecessors he maintained a private intelligence service. One of his leading agents was Christopher Urswick, who had helped to prevent Richard III from kidnapping Henry when he had been Henry Tudor.

Another leading agent of the period was Thomas Burton, 'the king's spy', who relentlessly hunted down enemies of the monarch. Burton encouraged citizens to betray their fellows by offering a reward of £20, together with half the value of the denounced man's goods, if any information volunteered led to someone being found guilty of treason or conspiracy.

When Henry VIII succeeded his father in 1509, he employed a series of ministers to keep him in touch with what was going on and assist him in preventing revolts. One of his principal agents in these matters was Thomas Cromwell, who became principal secretary to the ruler in 1534. Cromwell served his royal master energetically, seeking out sedition (the act of encouraging others to rebel) and discontent up and down the land. In his first year of office he had one revolutionary, known as the Maid of Kent, put to death, and many others were to follow.

Anyone who would not take the oath of supremacy, acknowledging the king, not the Pope, as head of the Church, was arrested. Many, including Bishop Fisher and Sir Thomas More, were executed. Thomas Cromwell moved slowly around the country like a great spider, listening, observing and striking.

9 Thomas Cromwell served his master Henry VIII in a number of capacities and helped to gather information which was used to close many monasteries. His downfall began when, in an effort to secure an alliance between England and Germany, he helped to arrange a marriage between Henry and Anne of Cleeves. He told his monarch that Anne was beautiful. When, too late to withdraw from the marriage, Henry discovered that his bride was far from lovely, he never trusted Cromwell again. The latter was arrested on a charge of high treason and executed in 1540

10 Robert Aske, seen here fixing a proclamation to the door of York Minister, was a Yorkshire lawyer and squire who led a movement against Henry VIII called 'The Pilgrimage of Grace for the Commonwealth'. He gathered an army of 30,000 men, but was persuaded by the king to disband it. Aske was later seized, dragged on a hurdle through the streets of York one July market day, and then hung in chains until he died

There were conspiracies everywhere throughout the king's reign, and almost every group had its traitor, ready and willing to betray the others. Confidential reports poured in on Cromwell, many of them dealing with the wealth of the monasteries. The principal secretary sent out his agents to check even further. When he had accumulated enough information he and Henry VIII moved in on the monasteries, closed many of them down and took their wealth for the royal treasury.

While the king was engaged in internal affairs, his overseas intelligence service languished. Ambassadors sent back as much information as they could obtain, and letters from foreign countries were sometimes intercepted and opened. There was, however, no systematic gathering of information.

Upon the death of Henry, his son Edward VI had a brief reign and then Mary Tudor came to the throne. Mary was a Catholic, unlike her father Henry VIII, and she set out to re-establish the Catholic faith in England. A reign of terror ensued, with Protestants hunted down and slaughtered for their religious beliefs.

Mary used every means at her disposal to discover Protestants. Agents were scattered among the people to listen and betray. One conspiracy, that of Sir Thomas Wyatt to remove some of the queen's advisers, was betrayed and put down. Agents of the queen forcibly stopped a messenger of the French ambassador and discovered from documents in his possession that the French had known all about the plot for months.

Mary died after a reign of only five years. She was succeeded by her half-sister, Elizabeth, a Protestant. Elizabeth was to build up the military and naval might of the country, and with it to establish a most efficient espionage service.

Further Reading——
Unstead, *The Medieval Scene* (Black).
Baker, *The Early Middle Ages* (Hutchinson).
Borer, *People Like Us* (Michael Joseph).
Salzman, *England in Tudor Times* (OUP).
Reeves, *The Norman Conquest* (Longman).
Norman and Pottinger, *Warrior to Soldier* (Granada).
Usherwood, *Britain, Century by Century* (David and Charles).

11 The Traitor's Gate of the Tower of London, on the River Thames. Through this gate passed many who were to be executed for treason. Perhaps the most famous prisoner to pass through the Traitor's Gate on the way to the executioner's block was Lady Jane Grey, who was put to death in 1554 by Queen Mary

3　The Great Spy

Upon the death of Mary, her half-sister Elizabeth became Queen of England. Elizabeth I was a Protestant. In the early years of her reign she was prepared to allow the Catholics in her realm to live at peace as long as they did not plot against her. There were, however, a number of plots and conspiracies and towards the end of her life Elizabeth dealt harshly with any Catholics who might be a danger to her throne. There were also grave threats from overseas, particularly from Spain and France. The queen was in great need of an efficient intelligence service, and thanks mainly to one man she got it.

The great spy – Francis Walsingham

The man who organised Elizabeth's secret service was Francis Walsingham. Born in 1530, Walsingham was a Protestant. While Mary's persecution of the Protestants was taking place in England, Walsingham quietly toured Europe. He was an observant man, possessed of great intelligence and a high degree of curiosity. He noted many things during his travels and quietly stored them away in his mind for future use.

When Elizabeth came to the throne Walsingham returned to England and offered his services to the queen's chief minister, Lord Burghley. The latter was impressed by the quiet and determined Walsingham and soon noticed how astute and tenacious he was. Taking into account Walsingham's recently acquired knowledge of the continent, the chief minister sent the young man abroad for several years to act as an agent, reporting back on any matters likely to be of interest to England.

Walsingham performed so well in this capacity that in 1569 he was called back to England in order to set up a secret service organisation for the queen. Before he could do more than begin this work he was diverted by an even more urgent need. Elizabeth and her advisers were afraid of the intentions of France. They needed constant, accurate information about what was going on in that country. Walsingham seemed just the man to provide this. He was sent to Paris as the British ambassador.

Like many other diplomats of the time, Walsingham was more of an agent than an ambassador. Conscientiously he set out to discover as much as he could about any French designs on England, and provided a steady flow of information back to his masters. But Walsingham was not happy with his position. Maintaining the embassy and paying a pack of spies and informers was an expensive business. It was not something that the ambassador could easily afford. With some relief he obeyed an order to return home in 1573.

12 Ambassadors, of the sort being received here by Elizabeth I, sent as much useful information as they could back to their own countries. In addition to keeping their own eyes open, many of them tried to employ Englishmen as their spies. Although the rewards for such treason were high, so were the penalties. Anyone found guilty of betraying his country was hanged, drawn and quartered

The queen and her councillors were pleased with Walsingham's work. He was made Secretary of State, in charge of the foreign policy of his monarch. Walsingham did more than maintain an interest in overseas affairs. He also built up an impressive spy ring at home. This gave him warning of any plots against the queen and later was to earn him the title of 'Father of the Secret Service'. In 1577 he was knighted for his work.

Before long Walsingham had developed a most effective system of spies and agents. He employed all sorts of people. Some of his agents worked for him because of their religious or patriotic principles. Others enjoyed the danger and excitement of their work. Many did it mainly for the money. Walsingham did not scruple to employ rogues and criminals if he thought that they could help him. He once said: 'if there were no knaves, honest men should hardly come by the truth of any enterprise against them'.

Some of Walsingham's spies were outstandingly successful. One of them was Antony Standen. Standen came from a Catholic family but had left the faith. Few people were aware of this and Standen was still welcome in many Catholic homes. He used this to make many contacts and gather a great deal of information.

One of Standen's most valuable pieces of work occurred when he became a friend of the Tuscan ambassador to Spain, Giovanni Figliazzi. At about the same time Standen also became acquainted with a member of the staff of the admiral in charge of the Spanish navy, Santa Cruz. With the information he received from both men Standen was able to provide Walsingham with an amazingly clear picture of the strength of the Spanish fleet and the intentions of the Spanish diplomats.

Walsingham used the information supplied by Standen and other agents and was able to report to Queen Elizabeth that the Spaniards would be in no position to attack England that year, especially if English ships were to raid Spanish ports and European financiers were discouraged from lending money to the Spaniards. Accordingly Elizabeth saw to it that Francis Drake launched a daring raid on Spanish vessels in Cadiz harbour and that the bankers of Genoa were informed that England would be very angry if money was given to the Spanish king to be used against England.

Another English agent, Richard Gibbs, also made investigations in Spain on Walsingham's behalf, posing as a Scot and an enemy of England. He reported that 300 Spanish vessels were waiting to invade England.

When the Spanish Armada finally did sail against England, Walsingham was well provided with information and saw to it that the English admirals were kept informed about the strength and position of the Spanish fleet. The English vessels were able to harry the larger Spanish galleons mercilessly and destroy many of them, driving off the Spanish for ever.

Walsingham was able to perform another great service to his monarch by keeping the Catholic Mary Queen of Scots, a claimant to the throne of England, under constant observation. Mary was the centre of a number of Catholic plots and eventually Walsingham's agents provided the information that led to her arrest and execution. Before that, one of Walsingham's agents had actually obtained work as a messenger for the Scottish queen, had copied all letters passing through his hands and had even obtained the details of a secret code being used by the queen's advisers.

Walsingham was always on the alert for possible traitors. In 1583, Sir Edward Stafford who was related to Elizabeth I, was made the English ambassador in Paris. Walsingham's agents were able to prove that Stafford had been accepting bribes from the Spanish. When confronted with this Stafford claimed that he had taken the money in order to gain the confidence of his country's enemies and obtain information from them.

Walsingham was extremely dubious about this explanation, but when Stafford provided him with information about the Spanish Armada he decided to keep his suspicions to himself as long as Stafford was removed from his embassy post and returned to England where he could no longer do any harm whilst the great spy's agents were watching him.

So the great spymaster continued on his way. His spies were quietly watchful. Little of any importance happened in England without it being reported back to their master. Men from all walks of life were eager to serve him, including such writers as Christopher Marlowe and Ben Jonson. He even prevailed upon the Lord Mayor of London to let him have weekly accounts of the movements of all foreigners in the capital.

Walsingham was also deeply interested in codes and cyphers. He realised how important it was to be able to transmit messages secretly. He urged his assistants to solve the codes being used by other powers. Some of these were very complex. One code devised by Blaise de Vigenère, a Frenchman, was still being used three hundred years later. Whenever he was needed, Walsingham was there to report the facts to his monarch in his usual quiet and unemotional manner. He did not exaggerate and he was always well-informed and reliable.

He could not always rely on the help and co-operation he deserved from Elizabeth I. Although honours were bestowed upon him and he became Chancellor of the Duchy of Lancaster, Walsingham was kept extremely short of funds and had to subsidise the secret service out of his own pocket, so much so that at his death in 1590 the great spy was a poor man.

Decline of the secret service

After the death of Walsingham the intricate spy network built up by the great spy at home and abroad was allowed to go into decline. Elizabeth I could find no-one of Walsingham's calibre to maintain the service and when she died her successor, James I, was even more reluctant to spend money on an intelligence system than Elizabeth had been.

One of Walsingham's assistants had been Thomas Phelippes, an expert on codes and cyphers. After the death of his master, Phelippes had retired from the secret service. However, while he was in retirement he heard rumours of a plot to blow up the Houses of Parliament while the king was there. Phelippes followed up these rumours, one of the first examples of a freelance agent conducting an investigation in Britain.

Phelippes's discoveries enabled him to warn the king's councillors and a watch was kept on some of the suspects. This surveillance, together with the inefficiency of the conspirators, led to the discovery of the Gunpowder Plot in 1605. A group of Catholics organised by a man called Catesby and including the famous Guy Fawkes had planned to blow up the Houses of Parliament and kill the king. Thirty barrels of gunpowder had been secreted in the cellars below the building

13 In this picture of Queen Elizabeth and her Parliament, Sir Francis Walsingham, the Secretary of State and the great Tudor spymaster, is seen standing at the Queen's left hand. He developed a most efficient counter-espionage service, often financing it out of his own pocket. His queen acknowledged his ability but did little to reward it, and Walsingham died a poor man

14 When an attempt to blow up the Houses of Parliament failed in 1605, the authorities arrested Guido (Guy) Fawkes, a soldier of fortune who was supervising the actual attempt. Fawkes was arrested, tortured and executed. The other conspirators seen in this picture all fled. They were pursued relentlessly. Some were killed. Others were arrested, brought to trial and then executed

for this purpose. The conspirators were arrested and executed.

Triumphs like these were few and far between for the counter-intelligence services in the reign of James I. One of the king's more successful spies was Sir Henry Wotton, the ambassador to Venice. Wotton was the wit who described the task of an ambassador as being to lie abroad for the good of his country.

James grudgingly allowed Wotton a small sum of money for intelligence purposes and the latter did his best to send back reports on the state of Europe as it affected England. He also controlled a surprisingly efficient intelligence service in England from his embassy in Venice. Wotton himself was not above accepting bribes and selling information to other powers, although he eased his conscience somewhat by taking money only from powers that were friendly towards Britain.

Spymaster Thurloe

Charles I, the successor to James, suffered from the poor state of the latter's secret service. Forced to rely upon dubious informers he was unable to obtain accurate and up-to-date reports of what was going on in the country. In 1642 when the people revolted against the monarch's despotic rule and the Civil War broke out, Charles was ill-prepared.

Throughout the Civil War spies and agents worked industriously for both the

... the battle of Naseby (1645). After this battle King Charles I surrendered to the Scots and the Civil War came to an end. The Scots handed Charles over to Parliament. The king was tried and, in 1649, he was executed

Puritans under Oliver Cromwell and the Royalists who supported the king. Neither side, however, had a really well-organised secret service and much depended upon the individual efforts of the agents concerned.

When the war ended with the defeat of the king, Cromwell became ruler of England. He realised the urgent need of a secret service system which would keep him informed since Royalists at home and overseas were plotting to put the House of Stuart back on the throne of Britain.

Cromwell chose wisely when he selected the head of his secret service. The man appointed was John Thurloe, a quiet lawyer who was dedicated to his master. In a short time Thurloe built the Lord Protector an intelligence service that was the envy of Europe. It was soon said of Oliver Cromwell that 'he carries at his girdle the secrets of all the princes of Europe'.

Cromwell gave Thurloe his complete trust and the almost unheard of sum of £70,000 a year to spend on his intelligence service. In return his spymaster was able to provide Cromwell not only with a massive spy network within Great Britain itself but he also scattered agents all over the continent. Thurloe was able to purchase the details of the most secret and confidential negotiations taking place abroad.

Most letters coming into the country from Royalists abroad or addressed to known sympathisers of the monarchy in Britain were intercepted and opened by Thurloe's agents. It was of little avail to the Royalists to use code. Thurloe employed Dr John Wallis, one of the most brilliant men of his time and a specialist in solving codes and cyphers.

Thurloe was very close personally to Cromwell. On one occasion the pair of them were in an accident together. The Lord Protector had been given a present of six horses. He harnessed them to a coach and they both went for a drive in Hyde Park. Unfortunately the horses bolted. Thurloe leapt from the coach, spraining his ankle, while Cromwell was pitched to the ground and dragged along behind the horses before the coach could be halted.

In addition to such accidents there were deliberate attempts on Cromwell's life, all of which had to be averted by Thurloe and his agents. Like Walsingham before him, the spymaster was prepared to employ anyone who could provide him with information or who could help to strike a blow against the Royalists lurking overseas.

Britain was divided into eleven areas, each under the control of an agent who had the rank of major general. It was the responsibility of each agent to see to it that there was no unrest in his section of the country and to report back quickly on any untoward events. While this meant that Thurloe was presented with a highly efficient spy network, the people of the country bitterly resented the local rule of the major generals, some of whom were cruel and oppressive.

Throughout Cromwell's reign as Lord Protector plots against the great man's life proliferated. Secret societies existed in abundance: the Levellers, the Fifth Monarchy Men, and many others. Cromwell was threatened by Royalists, religious fanatics, disgruntled Puritans, and some of his own ambitious generals. The Royalists in exile offered £500 a year to anyone who could kill the Lord Protector. There were uprisings in Wiltshire, the Midlands and the North of England. Thurloe and his men were constantly on the alert and received advance information about practically every serious attempt to disturb the peace or overthrow Cromwell.

Individuals who were convicted of plotting against the realm were dealt with swiftly and harshly. One would-be assassin, Miles Sindercombe, planned to kill Cromwell at the opening of Parliament. There were so many guards present at the occasion that he was unable to get near the Lord Protector. With dogged determination he began to follow the Lord Protector everywhere, waiting for his chance to strike. Thurloe's agents were too efficient so Sindercombe changed his plans. He decided to burn down Whitehall. Someone betrayed him to the authorities and he was arrested.

A former comrade-in-arms of the Protector, Colonel Sexby, was convicted of conspiring to encourage an uprising and was executed. Major Packer and six others accused of causing discontent within the army were dismissed and could count themselves fortunate to escape with their lives.

In 1658, a Royalist agent Dr John Hewitt, a former chaplain to Charles I, landed in Britain to foment a revolt. His presence was discovered by Thurloe's agents and the former chaplain was followed until he led Thurloe to his fellow-conspirators. When this had been accomplished, the plotters were arrested.

16 Oliver Cromwell was the chief leader of the Puritan Revolution in England. In 1653, he became Protector of the Commonwealth of England, Scotland and Ireland. He introduced a number of reforms, but was opposed by those who had supported King Charles before the latter's execution in 1649. Cromwell, however, had an efficient intelligence service and was able to put down any attempts to overthrow him

Hewitt and Sir Henry Slingsby, a Yorkshire squire, were put to death.

At Cromwell's insistence, agents began to hunt down women suspected of witchcraft. In one two-year period some two hundred women were executed. One of the chief persecutors of the so-called witches was Matthew Hopkins, who was himself later hanged as a sorcerer.

By constant vigilance and by the oppression of the people carried out by many of his representatives, Thurloe kept his master safe and in control of the country. After the Lord Protector's death in 1658, Thurloe continued to serve Cromwell's son Richard during the latter's brief period in office. It was at this time that the spymaster managed to destroy the Royalist society known as the Sealed Knot. Thurloe bribed Sir Richard Willis, one of the members of the secret society, to betray his fellows.

Fortunately for the Stuart cause, one of Thurloe's agents in his turn, sensing that the Royalists would soon be back in power in England, was able to warn Charles about the defection of Sir Richard Willis. Charles was therefore able to ignore any messages from the turncoat knight, and the plans Thurloe might have been entertaining to try and trap Charles had to be abandoned.

Later, when Charles returned to Britain as Charles II, he showed his admiration for the spymaster by continuing to consult him from time to time on matters of espionage. The king, being a practical man, was perfectly willing to forget that not long before the spymaster had been working against him. It was yet another example of the fact that a good spy was far too valuable to be wasted.

Further Reading——
Gittings, *Stuart People* (Hulton).
Garnett, *Know About the Armada* (Blackie).
Buchan, *Cromwell* (Hodder and Stoughton).
Deacon, *A History of the British Secret Service* (Muller).
Ross, *The English Civil War* (Faber).
Salzman, *English Life in the Middle Ages* (Batsford).
Millward, *The Sixteenth Century* (Hutchinson).
Unwin, *Crown and Parliament* (Black).

4 Spying Becomes a Profession

It was becoming increasingly obvious to those responsible for the security of Britain that it was no longer enough to rely for intelligence on the efforts of a handful of freelance agents. Some of these spies were inaccurate, others were prejudiced, most were for sale to the highest bidder. What was needed was a really well-organised, permanent secret service of the sort envisaged by Walsingham and later by Thurloe.

Other nations were coming to the same conclusion and Great Britain was suffering as a result. In France the chief minister, Cardinal Richelieu, built up a most impressive secret service from about 1630 onwards. A wealthy man, Richelieu paid his agents out of his own purse and they were loyal to him alone.

He soon had spies in the highest places in Britain. When Charles II returned from exile, the French saw to it that a beautiful woman spy, Louise de Kéroualle, came to London under the pretext of serving Charles's sister. The monarch fell in love with the glamorous agent, as Richelieu had hoped, and she became his mistress. Charles gave her the title of Duchess of Portsmouth. From her privileged position Louise de Kéroualle was able to send information back to Richelieu in France.

17 Cardinal Richelieu built up an espionage network throughout France, and also overseas. Next to the king he was the most powerful man in the country, and his influence over Louis XIII was enormous. Richelieu was also a most efficient general, and led the French armies with great success. The noblemen of France hated the powerful cardinal, but his spies were everywhere, and he was able to put down several revolts

18 Titus Oates being pilloried in the stocks. Surrounding him in this illustration are some of his victims. Oates persuaded the authorities that there was going to be a Catholic uprising in Britain. The Catholics, he swore, would kill as many Protestants as possible, burn London and help the French invade the country from Ireland. In the panic which followed, Oates was regarded as a saviour of his country, given a pension and a suite of apartments at Whitehall. Many Catholics, on his evidence, were imprisoned and executed. Eventually Oates was shown to be a rogue and liar. He was pilloried, flogged and sentenced to a term of imprisonment

Titus Oates

With so many people worried about the increasing power of the Catholics under the Stuarts, it was almost inevitable that sooner or later someone would attempt to use this anxiety to further their own ends. Such a person was Titus Oates, a rogue who masqueraded as a freelance undercover agent working for the good of his country. Oates pretended to have discovered a Catholic plot, known as the Popish Plot, in which the secretary of the king's brother was going to kill the king, help a French invasion of Britain and massacre all the Protestants.

Oates, the son of a clergyman, had had a checkered career. He had been expelled from school and a contemporary of his at Cambridge University had noted that 'he was a liar from the beginning'. For a time he was a clergyman in the Church of England, but resigned or was dismissed. He became a chaplain in the Royal Navy and was expelled. He then became, or pretended to become, a Roman Catholic.

Oates approached the Catholic Society of Jesus, also known as the Jesuits, and asked them for help. Twice the Jesuits sent Oates overseas to colleges in Spain and Flanders. Each time he was expelled. Back in London in 1678 he begged money from the Society. At the same time he was working on his plot to give false evidence against the Jesuits.

Oates published a pamphlet, *The Narrative of the Horrid Plot and Conspiracy*, in which he made his accusations against the Catholics in general and the Jesuits in particular. With the aid of an accomplice, Israel Tonge, he did his best to make known these charges. People were horrified by the so-called revelations; most of them believed everything that Oates said and the lives of Catholics everywhere were in danger. Oates and Tonge became popular heroes, Oates in particular being described as 'the saviour of the nation'. For a while Oates was a man of great importance. If he decided to accuse a Catholic of any crime, then that Catholic's life and reputation were both endangered. In the end, however, saner opinions prevailed. Oates was proved to be a liar. He was pilloried, whipped and imprisoned.

The end of the Stuarts

Although he had been welcomed back to England, before his death Charles II was at odds both with Parliament and his Protestant subjects. There were wars with the Dutch, aided by the French and the Danes, and Charles was accused of spending too much money on himself.

There was one plot to kidnap the king and his brother James as they returned from a race-meeting at Newmarket. By chance the king changed his plans and the conspiracy failed, but it was obvious to everyone that the royal intelligence service was a poor one, mainly because insufficient money was being spent on it.

Charles died in 1685 and he was succeeded by his brother, who became James II. After an uprising led by the Duke of Monmouth and put down with great slaughter, James dissolved Parliament and began to put Catholics into important positions. England was heading for civil war. William and Mary of Orange were invited to rule England and in 1689 William landed in Devon. James's followers deserted him and the king fled the country.

For the first half of the eighteenth century William and Mary and their successors to the throne of England were plagued by Jacobite plots at home and overseas. The followers of James II transferred their allegiance to his son and to his grandson, helping them to launch two invasions, one in 1715 and the other in 1745.

This meant that most of the efforts of the rudimentary intelligence services at first existing were directed to accumulating as much information as possible about the Jacobites. Apart from a few bribes handed out on their own initiative by various ambassadors little overseas espionage took place that was not concerned with thwarting the Jacobite cause. The detailed plans which were submitted for a more efficient secret service at the beginning of the eighteenth century came from a most unusual man.

Daniel Defoe

Daniel Defoe, who seems to have deserved the description most often accorded him, that of being a likeable rogue, was born the son of a London merchant. Before he was twenty-five years old he had taken part in the Duke of Monmouth's unsuccessful rebellion and had been very lucky to avoid the gallows afterwards. He married an heiress and with her dowry he went into business. The business failed, Defoe lost all his money and became bankrupt.

While he was still in his twenties Defoe discovered that in addition to a pleasant manner and a ready tongue he possessed considerable gifts as a writer. He was soon using these gifts in too impetuous a manner and was making enemies with the defamatory pamphlets issuing from his pen. One of these publications was the cause of Defoe being arrested and thrown into prison.

Throughout his life, however, Defoe managed to make friends in the right places. One of these friends was Robert Harley, Earl of Oxford and a very important man. Upon his release from prison Defoe submitted to Harley an extremely detailed plan for the formation of a new secret service organisation. Defoe argued that the government should be kept supplied with constant reports on all important areas, so that the state of the country could always be ascertained. Defoe also advocated that constant files should be maintained on all important people in each town and country area, so that the authorities would always know who was likely to be disaffected and thus a source of potential trouble. This seemed a good idea to Harley and he employed Defoe as an agent to see how useful he might prove. Defoe took to the work at once. With his inquisitive streak and his powerful imagination he showed that he could be most successful in hunting down Jacobites hiding in Britain.

In 1704 Harley made Defoe a principal secret agent and sent him on a tour of the country to provide the government with as much information as possible about the feelings of the ordinary people. Defoe travelled under the name of Alexander Goldsmith. On more than one occasion he was suspected of being a government spy and had to beat a hasty retreat. On the whole, however, he provided enough useful information to satisfy his masters.

Despite being kept short of money by Harley, Defoe also began to build up a network of agents as he had originally recommended. He received their reports and used them to build up an overall picture of the state of the country which he would report to the authorities accordingly.

In 1706 Defoe was sent to Edinburgh in connection with a matter which was causing the government much concern. This was the proposed union of the English and Scottish Parliaments, a most controversial issue. Defoe's delicate mission was not only to provide an accurate account of the feelings of the Scottish people, but also to persuade as many of them as possible that the forthcoming union would be a good thing for both countries.

It was a task fraught with danger for Defoe for had it been discovered that he was a government agent, the consequences would not have been pleasant for him.

19 Daniel Defoe was among those who wrote and published pamphlets criticising aspects of the Church and Government with which he disagreed. One pamphlet, entitled *The Shortest Way With Dissenters*, annoyed Queen Anne. Defoe was fined, put in the pillory and then imprisoned. He was released several years later, in 1704. He promptly founded a newspaper, wrote books and became a government spy

20 At the Battle of Culloden in 1746, the Duke of Cumberland led the English army against the invading Highland force under Charles Edward Stuart. The Scots were defeated with great slaughter, and Charles was forced to flee. Eventually he escaped to France. This was the last great effort of the Jacobites to gain power in Britain

But he rose to the occasion. Pretending to some that he was in the process of starting a small business, and to others that he was writing a book, Defoe mingled freely with Scots in all stations of life and persuasively encouraged them to support the union.

Defoe and his fellow agents did their job well and the union was accomplished. Harley and the other important men who were backing Defoe were well satisfied with his work. This did not make them any more generous and to the end of his days Defoe complained about the mean behaviour of his employers. However, in 1719 he wrote the famous *Robinson Crusoe*, and for a time at least his financial problems were eased.

The American War of Independence

The secret service organised by Daniel Defoe was expanded and continued to work fairly smoothly throughout the eighteenth century. It was assisted by the development of a military intelligence service under the control of the great English general, the Duke of Marlborough.

The English were aided during this period by one of the most unusual espionage agents who ever lived. This was a Frenchman, the Chevalier d'Eon de Beaumont. Often disguised as an attractive young woman, d'Eon used his wits and charm to extract secrets from high-ranking officials of both Russia and England. Eventually, however, he quarrelled with his superiors and came to England, bringing valuable information with him in return for shelter and protection.

Sir Robert Walpole, England's first Prime Minister, was eager that he should be kept well-informed. He encouraged the development of intelligence services until it could be said that 'no gun could be fired without Britain knowing why'.

Walpole's successor, William Pitt, also realised the importance of a well-organised secret service. He was particularly anxious to have up-to-date information about what was going on in the North American colonies. It had become apparent that the colonists were not satisfied with their lot and that there was a growing demand among them for independence.

The secret service managed to attach an agent to one of the most important of all the colonists, Benjamin Franklin, the American representative in Paris. The agent, Dr Edward Bancroft, was a very clever scientist who had invented a process of dyeing cloth. Franklin himself was very interested in scientific matters, and Bancroft became the American's friend and assistant. This meant that the spy was able to pass on to London details of all Benjamin Franklin's negotiations with

21 The Chevalier d'Eon was a most successful eighteenth-century spy. He often dressed up as a woman in order to obtain information. In fact many people were not sure whether he really was a man or a woman! After his death his body was dug up in order for an examination to be made

the French authorities. Bancroft also pretended to be spying for the American cause and handed over a great deal of worthless and misleading information to the Americans.

The colonists also had an espionage system, under the control of Arthur Lee. When the latter visited Berlin, however, his hotel room was broken into by the British ambassador in Berlin, Hugh Elliot, and his secret papers were copied and sent back to England, to the great satisfaction of the head of the secret service, Sir William Eden, although King George III was horrified at the action of his ambassador.

In 1775 the thirteen American colonies revolted against the rule of Great Britain and the War of Independence began. It was to continue until the colonists,

22 At the beginning of the American War of Independence, the forces of the American colonists occupied a commanding site on Bunker's Hill, overlooking the city of Boston. The British forces in Boston marched out to drive the colonists off the hill. However, they made their attack in broad daylight and were twice driven back. They finally succeeded in driving the colonists away. Eventually the British and their American loyalist allies were forced to evacuate Boston

View of The ATTACK on BUNKER'S HILL, with the Burning of CHARLES TOWN, June 17 1775.

aided by the French, finally defeated the British and achieved their sought-after freedom. During this war, fought on North American soil, spies abounded on both sides. The situation seemed made for them. Both sides spoke the same language; some of the colonists were sympathetic towards the British cause; and the lines of battle were constantly moving, leading to confusion and chaos. Under such conditions agents should have been able to work relatively freely and gather a great deal of information. In fact most attempts at military espionage were poorly planned, amateurish in their execution and usually ended in disaster for those taking part.

One of the best-known spies on the side of the colonists was Nathan Hale, who became famous not so much for what he did as for what he said. He was not a very successful spy but his final words on the scaffold after his capture have been handed down to posterity as an example of courage and patriotism.

Nathan Hale was born in Connecticut in 1755, one of twelve children of a prosperous farmer. He had a normal childhood, excelling at games and athletics, and received his early education from a local clergyman. At the age of fourteen he entered the university of Yale, and after he had graduated he became a schoolteacher. There was nothing at all remarkable about this young man, except for his deep love of his country, and had it not been for the war he would probably have spent the rest of his life quietly as a country schoolmaster.

When the war broke out, Nathan Hale enlisted in the Revolutionary Army and became a lieutenant. He took part in the successful siege of Boston and was promoted to the rank of captain. During the initial stages of the war both sides suffered reverses. After a defeat at the Battle of Long Island, the American leader, George Washington, desperately wanted to know where the British troops were. Nathan Hale volunteered to become a spy for the occasion and to discover as much as he could about the enemy position.

Accordingly the young man put on civilian clothes and crossed over to Long Island, mingling with the British troops he found there. He made maps and took notes about the positions of the soldiers and artillery that he could see. Unfortunately for him, while he was still near the enemy camp the British made a sudden attack on the colonists and drove them back to Harlem. This meant that the Americans were now much further away than they had been when Hale had left them to infiltrate the enemy lines.

Hurriedly the youth tried to make his way back to safety, but he was captured and taken before General Howe, the leader of the British army. It was useless for Hale to deny that he had been spying. The maps and notes on his person gave him away. The young captain admitted who he was and what he had been doing and General Howe ordered his execution.

On the following morning, 22 September at 11 am, Nathan Hale was hanged. Before his execution he made his celebrated declaration: 'I only regret I have but one life to give for my country'. It is possible that the words were adapted from a play by a writer called Addison, but Nathan Hale gave them new life and they are still remembered and quoted today.

Espionage at a much higher level occurred several years later. It involved one of the most popular generals of the Army of the Revolution, Benedict Arnold. Arnold was a very fine soldier and a man of great charm and personality. He was much loved by his troops and his defection to the enemy came as an enormous shock to the Americans.

Even as a child Benedict Arnold had wanted to be a soldier. Twice he had run away from home to join the British army fighting against the French and their Red Indian allies in North America. Later he made an attempt to settle down and became a merchant in New Haven. But his love of the army continued and he joined the Connecticut militia. This was a band of spare-time soldiers who trained and drilled in the evenings and at the week-ends. Upon the outbreak of war Benedict Arnold joined the army of the colonists and fought bravely and with great flair against the British. He reached the rank of major general and was placed in charge of the fortress of West Point.

It was then that Arnold turned traitor and began to spy for Britain. The reasons for his amazing duplicity are still not clear. Arnold certainly liked to live well and expensively, and he was often in debt; the money offered by the British may have been sufficient to make him betray his country. He was also an impatient and ambitious man who suspected that certain episodes in his past made his superiors reluctant to promote him as quickly as he deserved. Whatever the cause of his actions, Benedict Arnold began to send military information secretly to the British, the enemies of his country. Sometimes his wife acted as a messenger for him.

The British were delighted to be receiving so much secret information from the colonists. They wanted even more. With Arnold in charge of West Point it should be possible for the American general to throw open the gates of his fortress and surrender it to the British. Sir Henry Clinton, commander of all the British land forces in North America, was particularly anxious to accomplish this.

In an effort to persuade Arnold to betray West Point, Sir Henry Clinton sent one of his young officers to negotiate secretly with the general. The officer selected was Major John André. André was a handsome, witty young man who had joined the army after an unhappy love affair. He proved to be a good soldier and rapidly won promotion. As soon as it had been ascertained that Benedict Arnold was willing to discuss giving up West Point to his enemies the major set out to meet the general.

On 20 September 1780, André sailed up the River Hudson on the sloop *Vulture*. He went ashore and met Arnold by night in a house near Stony Point. While the two men were discussing the details of the proposed surrender at some length, a battery of American guns on the shore spotted the *Vulture* and opened fire. The sloop was forced downstream and was unable to pick up Major André for the return voyage.

Persuaded that his only hope of returning to New York was by donning civilian

23 The handsome and talented John André, an officer in the British Army during the American War of Independence, was hanged as a spy in 1780. His execution aroused a great deal of protest. André had merely been acting as a go-between negotiating with the American General Benedict Arnold who was thinking of handing over West Point to the British. George Washington, the American leader, refused to see André before the latter's death, or to issue orders for the execution to be halted

clothes, with some reluctance André did so. He then set out to try and return to New York on horseback. On 23 September, three American militiamen stopped him near Tarrtown and asked the major to give an account of himself. In the confusion André thought at first that the men confronting him were British soldiers and he gave away his true identity. When he realised that he had been stopped by Americans André tried to bluff his way out of the situation. It was too late. The Americans searched him and found incriminating papers in his pockets.

André was arrested and taken to George Washington's headquarters at Tappan. The American leader refused to see the prisoner but ordered an immediate military court martial. The major was found guilty of espionage and sentenced to death.

There was a great deal of sympathy for the condemned Englishman, on the American side as well as the British. Many felt that André had been a scout or an emissary rather than a spy, and that the real agent was Benedict Arnold. General Washington ignored all pleas for clemency, and on 2 October Major André was hanged.

The opinions of many people were summed up in a piece of contemporary verse:

André was executed
He looked both meek and mild
His face was fair and handsome
And pleasantly he smiled
It moved each eye with pity
And every heart there bled
And every one wished him released
And Arnold in his stead

Benedict Arnold, however, escaped. By chance he had heard of André's arrest soon after it had taken place and the general managed to flee to the safety of the British lines. There he was welcomed and rewarded. The British gave him a sum of about £6,000 and put him in command of a body of troops.

For the remainder of the war Arnold led a series of daring raids against his fellow countrymen, but with the final defeat of the British he had to leave North America and live in Great Britain. He failed to obtain a commission in the British army, and a number of trading ventures failed. He died in 1801, a disappointed man.

Disturbed and annoyed by the failure of his agents, George Washington decided to place his espionage service under the command of Major Benjamin Tallmadge. Although he had had no previous experience of secret service work the major managed to bring some sort of order to the colonists' spy system. He chose his agents carefully and made sure that only he was aware of their true identity. He scattered his spies about the country in a number of guises—as store-keepers, travelling school-teachers, and so on. Thanks to Tallmadge's efforts and the willingness of Washington to spend money on his intelligence service, the Americans ended the war with a far more effective espionage service than they began it.

Jack the Painter

While the War of Independence was being fought in North America, the French and the colonists were encouraging agents in Great Britain to cause as much trouble as possible to the British war effort. One of their most effective methods was to sabotage the ships in British harbours and dockyards.

In 1776 there were outbreaks of fire in the dockyards of Portsmouth and Bristol. The authorities were sure that the same methods of starting the fire had been used in each case and that the same agent may have been responsible for each blaze.

A contemporary magistrate's poster described the man in question. He was called John and he was a painter by trade. He was about twenty-five years old, five feet seven inches (160 centimetres) tall, fair complexioned and with sandy hair. A reward of £50 was offered for his capture; this sum was to be given to the man himself if 'knowing himself to be innocent' he voluntarily appeared before Commissioner Gambier at Portsmouth.

This wanted enemy agent captured the public's imagination. He became the subject of songs and stories sold in the street, under the name of 'Jack the Painter'. The man's real name turned out to be James Hill, and he was not a very efficient agent nor saboteur, being captured quite easily. It transpired that he had been bribed by the American ambassador to France to create as much havoc as possible in British dockyards. He appeared before a court at Winchester on 6 March 1777, charged with that he 'did maliciously set on fire and burn in the rope-house, twenty tons of hemp, of the value of £100, ten cable ropes, each one hundred fathoms in length and valued at £80, and six tons weight of cordage valued at £200, besides damage beyond compare to the dockyard'.

24 (*Left*) It was not difficult to obtain information about shipping movements in British seaports. Ladies of the town were always waiting to meet seamen returning home with money in their pockets. In the eighteenth century there was an outbreak of fires in dockyards up and down the country. Arsonists had no difficulty finding their way into the dockyards to start their blazes

25 (*Right*) Before the introduction of an efficient police force, some semblance of law and order was maintained in the streets of large cities by night watchmen. These men were poorly paid and not very efficient. This illustration shows the contempt with which 'the guardians of the night' were regarded. Thieves are breaking into a house, a building appears to be on fire, but the watchman plods on, ignoring everything

The story which came out at the trial showed the poor quality of the agents the French and Americans were forced to employ. Hill had arrived at a Portsmouth lodging house on 6 December 1776, having obtained employment in the dockyard as a labourer. He had left the house for a short while and an inquisitive landlady had gone through his belongings, finding among them a suspicious tin canister of the sort sometimes used for home-made bombs.

Hill's attitude had aroused suspicion from the start. He had asked one fellow lodger if there was a way of escaping over the city wall, pretending to be afraid of

43

being recruited by a naval press-gang. Later that same evening Hill got drunk and boasted to another lodger that he had spied on all the dockyards of England and that he had made several trips to Paris to give these facts to the American ambassador there.

The next day huge clouds of black smoke were seen billowing out of Hill's room. He had been experimenting with his fire-lighting apparatus. The landlady promptly gave the man notice and sent him packing. That same day the fire broke out in the rope-house at the dockyard.

When Hill was arrested there was found on his person a pamphlet on the starting of fires, a loaded pistol and a French passport under an assumed name. The jury found Hill guilty without leaving the room. He was sentenced to death. On 10 April 1777 he was hanged at the dock gate at Portsmouth. First he was taken round the scene of the fire in an open cart. Hill surveyed the scene and said 'I acknowledge my crime and am sorry for it'. He warned the crowd that further arson and sabotage threatened the naval ports of Chatham, Deptford and Plymouth. Just before he was hanged he said 'I acknowledge the justice of my sentence and hope for forgiveness, as I forgive all the world'.

Further Reading——
Whittle, *Great Prime Ministers* (Black).
Harrison, *The Seventeenth Century* (Allen and Unwin).
Connell, *The Plains of Abraham* (Hodder and Stoughton).
Nye and Morpurgo, *A History of the United States* (Pelican).

5   An Abundance of Spies

By the end of the eighteenth century it would have been difficult to find a European nation, large or small, which did not possess an organised, full-time espionage service. Frederick the Great of Prussia declared 'I am always preceded by a hundred spies', and to a greater or lesser extent this boast could be echoed by most military leaders of the period.

Espionage becomes organised

In Great Britain, William Pitt and the Prime Ministers who followed him realised that international diplomacy was too complicated and internal affairs too uncertain to do without an organised spying system.

The outbreak of the French Revolution in 1789 gave Britain ample opportunity to meddle in the affairs of her old enemy and to create even more disorder. Throughout the revolution British agents permeated France. After it was over the British encouraged the exiled royalists to meet in Britain and plan to return in force to their country.

There was also much work for counter-espionage agents within Britain. Towards the end of the century ships of the navy mutinied at Spithead, the sailors demanding more pay and better conditions. The mutiny eventually ended and the ringleaders were punished, but the government was badly shaken. At first it was thought that the mutiny had been engineered by foreign agents, and British counter-espionage agents flooded the naval towns trying to track down these spies. It was later accepted that the mutiny had been a genuine one, inspired by the sailors themselves.

Some British agents were not above encouraging people to say disloyal things or commit treasonable acts and then promptly arresting them. Such agents were called *agents provocateurs*, and were feared and despised.

The man who caused the British the most concern, however, was the young French general, Napoleon Bonaparte. In the aftermath of the French Revolution Bonaparte showed himself to be a most able military leader, and soon he was leading the armies of a revitalised France against most of the powers of Europe.

The Napoleonic Wars

While Napoleon was conquering most of Europe and threatening Britain, secret services on both sides were busy at work. The British government encouraged the French royalists, exiled in London, to plot against Napoleon and make plans to restore Louis XVIII to the throne of France. A special training camp for spies and terrorists was situated at Romsey.

26 In the eighteenth century the authorities were worried about the printing of books and pamphlets which criticised the government and members of the royal family. They regarded such books as subversive, that is likely to make people despise the government. Attempts were made to stop the distribution of some of these publications. This caused an uproar among the people, many of whom objected to such censorship. This cartoon shows the authorities trying to prevent free speech. Part of an accompanying verse describes the attitudes of officials to these pamphlets:
> 'Oh! they are full of blasphemies and libels
> And people read them oftener than their Bibles.'

OF LITTLE BOOKS,

Pitt and his ministers encouraged several attempts on Napoleon's life. One was launched in December 1800. Three French royalists, Limoelan, Saint-Rejant and Carbon, arrived in Paris from London. Their intention was to kill Napoleon. They filled a cask with gunpowder and rocks, fixed a fuse to the contraption and loaded it on to a cart. They then took the cart to a street on a route they knew Napoleon's coach would take.

The intention was that Limoelan would take up a position some way in front of the cart and as soon as he saw Napoleon's coach he would signal to Saint-Rejant. Saint-Rejant would light the fuse and all three of them would flee. The cask would explode, destroying Napoleon's coach.

In the event, when the coach was seen approaching, Limoelan's courage failed him and he did not give the agreed signal. This left Saint-Rejant very little time in which to light the fuse. However, in the few seconds he had left he did so and then ran for his life.

Napoleon's coachman saw the cart blocking most of the street. If he had stopped it would have given the fuse time to burn down and the cask would have exploded just a few yards from Napoleon. Instead the coachman saw a narrow gap and whipping up his horses he drove the coach through the gap at a great pace, just squeezing past the cart. The coach reached the safety of the next street before the cask exploded. Napoleon was shaken and furious, but the three agents managed to escape the efforts of the French to hunt them down and arrest them.

The most important developments in espionage during the Napoleonic Wars were those involving military espionage and intelligence. Hitherto military intelligence had been rudimentary, but both Napoleon and the Duke of Wellington did much to improve this aspect of warfare.

As early as 1803 the British military authorities were planning a professional intelligence section to be known as the Depot of Military Knowledge. This section was to be responsible for collecting information, making maps and so on. Before much could be done, war with France broke out again.

In 1810, the Duke of Wellington was fighting the French in Spain. The general found it difficult to obtain accurate information about the enemy so he used 'exploring officers', whose duty it was to find out as much as they could about the French positions.

From this relatively small beginning an efficient military intelligence service developed. One of the 'exploring officers', Colquhoun Grant, showed great aptitude for the work and eventually became the first head of a British military intelligence service in the field. In Spain, working under the Duke of Wellington, Grant developed the intelligence service by using the reports of 'exploring officers', interviewing guerrillas, deserters, escaped prisoners of war and the ordinary civilian population; and by carefully reading as many European newspapers as possible in case any news of the French movements leaked out by mistake.

Grant made many expeditions behind the enemy lines in order to obtain information. Eventually he was caught. He escaped and actually made his way to Paris where he lived for nine months before returning to England.

Wellington was delighted by the initiative and courage displayed by Grant and in 1813 made him the head of his intelligence service. Grant did a great deal to provide Wellington with accurate information before the Battle of Waterloo.

With the defeat and exile of Napoleon many British officers were forced to leave the army. Grant, in spite of all his good work, was one of these. He existed on half-pay for four years before he was able to rejoin the colours. He fought in Burma and died in 1829 at the age of 48. After the Napoleonic Wars he was never given a chance to develop the military intelligence service he had done so much to instigate.

Napoleon's spy service was much more far-reaching than that of the Duke of Wellington, and he enjoyed the services of two excellent spymasters, Fouché and Schulmeister.

Joseph Fouché, a former ambassador to the Netherlands, became Minister of Police in France at the beginning of the nineteenth century. He built up an intricate spy network within the country and was soon a well-informed and powerful man. So influential did he become that Napoleon himself was worried and in 1802 the spymaster was dismissed. However, Napoleon discovered that he needed the services of someone as devious as Fouché, so after two years he was reinstated. He remained in charge of the French espionage service until 1810. Then his love of intrigue got the better of him and Napoleon decided that he could trust his agent no more. Again Fouché was dismissed and this time he did not return to power.

The Special Branch

As the nineteenth century progressed there was a growing demand in Great Britain for some sort of protection against the increasing waves of terrorism being directed against prominent people, especially in London. People demanded an

27 (*Left*) Leon Gambetta proclaiming the French Republic in September 1870. The following month Paris was besieged by the Germans. Gambetta managed to escape by balloon from the French capital but continued to lead the fight against the German invaders

28 (*Right*) In 1829, Sir Robert Peel brought in a bill 'for Improving the Police in and near the Metropolis'. The object of the Home Secretary's bill was to introduce a unified police force, first in London, and then throughout the country if possible. Constables recruited under this scheme were known as 'Peelers' after Sir Robert. They were paid 19 shillings (95p) a week later raised to 21 shillings (£1.05) a week, and provided with a free blue uniform of the sort shown above

efficient counter-espionage system which would hunt down the plotters and arrest them. These attacks were usually caused by agents working for foreign powers or by fanatics plotting to overthrow the government.

One of the first attempts was made by a revolutionary called Arthur Thistle-wood, who wanted to make himself dictator. In 1820 he gathered together a force of about 30 men. They laid elaborate plans to kill all the members of the British Cabinet and then seize power for themselves. It was decided to make the assassination attempt as the ministers were dining one evening at the home of Lord Harrowby.

The plot was hatched in the loft of a stable in Cato Street, and the affair later became known as the Cato Street Conspiracy. As was often the case when a large number of conspirators were involved, rumours of the meetings began to circulate. A freelance agent called Edwards, who made a living by selling information to the magistrates, managed to join the plotters and was able to report the full details to the authorities.

A number of Bow Street Runners, precursors of the police force, were sent to arrest Thistlewood and his gang. Unfortunately the attempt was bungled and fourteen of the conspirators escaped. In the confusion Thistlewood killed one of the Bow Street Runners with his sword. He was caught the following day. He and the other plotters were convicted of treason and murder and were hanged.

Other plots and a number of riots were a feature of the nineteenth century. A professional police force was established, but the police were concerned mainly with the prevention of ordinary crime. There was no body responsible for counter-espionage, the tracking down of enemy agents or those engaged in treasonable activities.

The Irish were causing particular trouble in England. Many of the Irish felt that their country should be independent. Secret societies were formed to fight against the English. One society was known as the Irish Black Legion, but the most effective organisation was known as the Fenians. Members of this group came over to England and tried to instigate a reign of terror. They planted bombs in buildings and blew up many of them, injuring a large number of people.

It was decided to form an organisation within the police force which would deal only with the Fenians and other Irish revolutionaries. The organisation was called the Special Irish Branch, commanded by Chief Inspector Kittlewood.

29 In 1867 a daring attack on a prison van was made in Manchester by the Fenians, Irishmen seeking freedom for their country. The van had been taking some of the leaders of the movement to prison, but their comrades attacked the horse-drawn vehicle and rescued them

30 A bomb planted by Fenians at New Scotland Yard destroyed an office, part of a public house and two carriages. This was just one of a number of acts of sabotage carried out by the Irish in English cities in the 1860s and 1870s

The formation of the SIB did not deter the Fenians. They even placed a bomb in Scotland Yard, the headquarters of the London police force. The bomb exploded, killing no-one but destroying an office. Another bomb was left on London Bridge and exploded as many workmen were crossing it on their way home.

Here the SIB had its first success. Officers discovered that a rowing boat was missing from a boat-house near by. The boat had been hired out to some men carrying a parcel only a short time before the bomb had exploded on the bridge. Suspicion fell upon two Irishmen whom the police had been watching for some time. These men were never found but the police were sure that when the bomb had exploded it had killed the conspirators in the rowing boat at the same time.

Other explosions followed, including ones at an underground station, the Tower of London and the House of Commons. The SIB was heavily criticised in its early days for its lack of success in apprehending the men responsible for the explosions. Slowly the organisation began to get to grips with the problem and the exploits of the Fenians grew less daring and less successful and eventually came to an end altogether.

By this time the efficiency of the Special Irish Branch was generally recognised. It was decided at Scotland Yard not to wind up the organisation even though the Irish problems seemed to have ended, at least for the time being. Instead the organisation was retained as a separate arm of the police force to deal with counter-espionage and similar matters. The word Irish was dropped from the title and the body was known simply as the Special Branch.

In the closing decades of the nineteenth century and during the early years of the twentieth century there was plenty of work for the Special Branch. Groups of revolutionaries were springing up all over Europe, their aim being to bring down organised society, by force if necessary. Such groups as the Anarchists and the Nihilists had outposts in most capital cities.

The Anarchists were particularly dangerous. In England they were found to have established a factory in which they were manufacturing bombs. They were going to use these bombs in an effort to overthrow authority in Great Britain. The Special Branch moved in and a number of arrests were made. In 1894, two Italians, Ferrara and Polti, were tried in London for plotting to blow up the Stock Exchange. Both men were found guilty and sentenced to long terms of imprisonment. Another revolutionary attempted to blow up Greenwich Observatory, but the bomb exploded in his hands, killing him.

Groups like the Anarchists and Nihilists were not all the Special Branch had to deal with. In an era of general discontent with poor living conditions and dreadful poverty for masses of people, there were numerous organisations trying to better the lot of working-class people, some of them prepared to use violence. The beginning of the twentieth century, for example, saw the efforts of the Suffragettes to obtain equal rights for women in Great Britain. Some women chained themselves to railings; others led protest marches; one even threw herself in front of a horse owned by the King when it was running at a race-meeting, killing herself in the process.

London was full of revolutionaries, including such famous thinkers and philosophers as Lenin and Karl Marx. All of them had to be kept under constant observation by the Special Branch in case they should start any trouble in Great Britain.

A particularly worrying time for the Special Branch came in 1910. King Edward VII died and his funeral was held in London. Royalty from all over Europe came to London to attend the funeral. It was an ideal opportunity for troublemakers who might have tried to assassinate some of the kings and princes present. Fortunately the event passed off without incident, but the Special Branch had taken enormous precautions.

A year later the police were less successful. A gang of revolutionaries who had killed three policemen were besieged in a house in Sidney Street in the East End of London. Thousands of people gathered to witness the scene as the men in the house exchanged shots with police and soldiers. Suddenly flames were seen coming from the house. Within a short time it had burned to the ground. The charred

31 In 1911, a gang of anarchists was trapped in Sidney Street in the East End of London. A detachment of Scots Guards, several hundred armed police and even a detachment of the Royal Horse Artillery turned out to lay siege to the gang. Thousands of people crowded the streets to witness the battle, and Winston Churchill, the Home Secretary, even arrived to direct operations for a time

corpses of two men were found in the ruins of the building, but the police suspected that the leader of the gang, known as Peter the Painter, had somehow escaped in the confusion.

Further Reading——
Huisman, *Stories of the French Revolution* (Burke).
Dumpleton, *Law and Order* (Black).
Gribble, *The Old Bailey* (Muller).
Morey, *Wellington* (Muller).
Jarman, *Socialism in Britain* (Gollancz).
Richards, *Britain 1714–1851* (Longman).
Wymer, *Social Reformers* (OUP).

6 The Great Game

Not all British espionage and counter-espionage activities took place in Europe. With the expansion of the British Empire it became necessary to have intelligence services in many corners of the world where the European powers were disputing over colonial possessions.

Such work attracted an unusual type of agent. Often they were gifted amateurs, men who did the work for the excitement and for the sheer love of 'the great game', as they called it. Sometimes they were employed by the Colonial Office or India Office, occasionally they were recruited by local ambassadors or political agents; a few were army officers granted leave to undertake some particularly dangerous spying mission in Africa or Asia.

Sir Richard Burton

Perhaps the most famous of all the wandering eccentric British agents was the explorer Richard Burton, who spent a lifetime travelling through unknown parts of the globe, studying local customs, writing books and reporting back on anything he thought might be of interest and importance to his country.

After a university education, Burton became a cadet in the Indian army in 1842. He displayed a sympathy for and understanding of the local way of life, and developed a gift for learning languages. He became an assistant in a survey of a huge area known as Sind and spent many months wandering among the people, learning their customs and traditions.

His superiors made use of his courage and enthusiasm. Burton was often sent out on missions to discover what was happening among the Indians. The subaltern would disguise himself as an Indian and live among the people. On one occasion he opened a store in Karachi, and while posing as a merchant gathered a great deal of information about what was going on from the bazaars of the city.

Burton was never able to settle down for long. He travelled extensively, often disguised as a native of the area he was exploring. Between 1851 and 1853, he made a pilgrimage to Mecca. He assumed a number of different disguises because if he had been revealed as a European and a Christian he would have been put to death. One of his names adopted on the perilous trip was Al-Haj Abdullah.

Burton's life was an adventurous one. He explored Somaliland, served in the Crimean War, took part in an expedition to discover the sources of the River Nile, and was British consul in charge of several areas. His personality, eccentric manner of living and outspoken opinions did not endear him to everyone and he made enemies, but as an agent in little-known areas of the world he was unsurpassed.

32 In 1853, Richard Burton shaved his head and grew a long beard. He stained his skin and set off on a pilgrimage to Mecca, dressed in flowing robes and assuming the name Mirza Abdulla ('Servant of Allah'). He could speak fluent Arabic but his trip was a dangerous one. Had he been discovered as an Englishman, he would have been put to death

The North-West frontier and beyond

One of the most romantic areas in which the great game was played was in the region of the North-West frontier of India and beyond into Afghanistan and Persia. In this dangerous and unsettled region both the British and the Russians strove for supremacy, playing off the tribesmen against each other. Although nominally at peace, agents of Britain and Russia were constantly at work in this no-man's land.

One of the most unusual of the British agents in this part of the world in the nineteenth century was McMorrough Kavanagh. Kavanagh travelled extensively in India and Persia, narrowly escaping death on a number of occasions while gathering material for his reports. His exploits were made even more remarkable by the fact that Kavanagh possessed neither arms nor legs. He had to be strapped into the saddle of his horse, wrote by gripping a pen between his teeth and defended himself with a specially-constructed shot-gun which he fired with the stump of one of his arms.

But even before Kavanagh was making his fantastic journeys across the continents men were working for Britain in Persia and India. Three of them were to meet in strange circumstances in Bokhara in 1844. The names of these three players of the great game were Colonel Charles Stoddart, Captain Arthur Conolly and Dr Joseph Wolff. All three were remarkable men, even by the standards of the time and their profession.

By the 1840s Central Asia had become important. The British on one side in India and Afghanistan, and the Russians on the other, were slowly advancing on each other across the intervening area. Small states like Bokhara suddenly assumed great strategic importance and their rulers were being wooed by both

British and Russian emissaries. Some of the rulers, however, did not particularly want to be wooed.

In 1838, Colonel Stoddart was sent on the long perilous journey to Bokhara to assure the Emir Nasrullah, the head of the state, that Britain had only the friendliest of intentions towards his country. Nasrullah was not impressed. Stoddart had insulted him by bringing no presents, and in any case Bokhara wanted nothing to do with distant foreign powers. Without ceremony Stoddart was seized, bound and imprisoned.

The colonel was not put to death and sometimes he was released and allowed to live quite comfortably. For much of the time, however, he was kept under dreadful conditions. All requests and demands for his release were ignored. After considerable thought the British authorities allowed a dashing and impetuous young officer named Conolly to make his way to Bokhara to attempt to secure Stoddart's release. Conolly was a brave young man but no diplomat, and the Emir imprisoned him as well.

It was then that the third and most eccentric of the agents appeared. This was Joseph Wolff, a talkative, stubborn and courageous Bavarian who had taken up residence in Great Britain and become a clergyman after years of wandering around Central Asia as a missionary.

Wolff had been moved by stories of the plight of Conolly and Stoddart and resolved to do his best to rescue the two officers. It was an incredible scheme, but friends of the imprisoned men raised enough money for his journey and the clergyman calmly set off for Bokhara and whatever he would find there.

Wolff actually reached the country and even met Conolly and Stoddart, but only in time to see them both executed as spies. Wolff, too, was imprisoned, but so persuasive a talker was he that he was soon released and allowed to wander around. On one occasion he attempted to escape but was recaptured and imprisoned. Instead of being condemned to death, the puzzled and impressed Emir, not knowing what to make of the incredible doctor, released him. After an adventurous journey Wolff reached the safety of Constantinople. He returned to England and for the remainder of his life lived as a country parson in Somerset.

Robert Baden-Powell

Many other agents followed in the footsteps of Kavanagh, Wolff and Burton, but theirs was a profession that could only be followed in primitive and unsophisticated surroundings. With the development of modern communications and techniques it became increasingly difficult for one man to accomplish as much as some of the earlier agents in the less well-known areas of the world.

One of the last of the great individual agents of this type was Robert Baden-Powell, who became famous later as the founder of the Scout and Guide movements. He was a professional soldier, a solitary, unusual man whose main hobby was amateur dramatics, although he was also a talented artist. From his early days in the army Baden-Powell realised that a thorough knowledge of an enemy

55

33 At the outbreak of the Boer War the British South African Police, seen here riding to relieve Mafeking in 1900, had to guard British interests in South Africa until troops could be sent out. At one time only 30 policemen, under Colonel Plummer, stood between the advancing Boers and their objective

was essential in order to be able to defeat him. He was convinced that Britain's main adversary would one day be Germany.

Accordingly the young officer spent his periods of leave at his own expense in Germany or in German territory in North Africa and elsewhere. Sometimes he would pretend to be a journalist, on other occasions he would take a sketch-pad with him and appear to be an artist. In reality he was studying the German troops and their weapons. Once he was caught and arrested near a secret military establishment, but he pretended to be drunk and the guards released him.

As a soldier Baden-Powell served in a number of campaigns. In 1876 he fought in India. His duties included going out on solitary missions, and it was here that he developed many of the ideas he was later to introduce into the Scout movement. He also fought in campaigns in Zululand, Ashanti and Matabeleland. Between 1891 and 1893 he was the intelligence officer for the Mediterranean area. It was not until the Boer War in South Africa at the turn of the century that he became famous.

34 Mafeking was relieved on 17 May 1900. Baden-Powell, the defender of Mafeking, is greeting Colonel Mahon, leader of the relieving force. Before they had made contact, Mahon had sent a message by heliograph asking 'How are you getting on?' Baden-Powell had answered simply 'Welcome'

56

When Baden-Powell went out to help put down the rising by the Boers he was an unknown lieutenant colonel of 42. He was given the task of organising the defence of the town of Mafeking. In a short time the town was surrounded by Boers and everyone thought that Baden-Powell would be forced to surrender in a very short time.

Instead he held out for 217 days, until 17 May 1900, when the town was relieved by another British force. During those 217 days Baden-Powell and his men attracted the attention of the whole of Britain by their courage and ingenuity. After the first Boer bombardment of the town Baden-Powell sent a telegram to London which read: 'All well. Four hours' bombardment. One dog killed'. The casual nature of the message appealed to the British public and Baden-Powell became their hero.

During the defence of Mafeking he organised elaborate espionage systems, sending scouts through the enemy lines. He had an intricate system of trenches and forts constructed. He sent messages over a loud-speaker system to non-existent troops to give the impression that his force was larger than it really was.

When the town was relieved and Baden-Powell returned to England he was extremely well-known. Many of his exploits formed material upon which he founded the Scout movement.

End of the game
With the approach of the twentieth century the great game came to an end. There seemed little room for the gentlemen adventurers who had ridden into unknown parts of Asia and Africa. The world was approaching the most savage war it had ever known.

Further Reading——
Reader, *Life in Victorian England* (Batsford).
Woodruff, *The Men Who Ruled India* (Cape).
Maclean, *A Person from England* (Cape).
Gallagher and Robinson, *Africa and the Victorians* (Macmillan).
Kruger, *Good-bye Dolly Gray: The Story of the Boer War* (Cassell).

7 Spies in the First World War

The twentieth century opened with the major powers of Europe jockeying for position. Military forces were being built up and espionage was becoming a regulated and highly-organised profession. The armed forces assumed responsibility for the secret service in both France and England.

MI5

In the first decade of the twentieth century the government recognised the fact that it was highly likely that Germany and other powers were sending spies to England. It was time that an organisation was formed to hunt down and capture these agents. This organisation should be under the general supervision of the military but should be allowed considerable freedom of action. The Committee of Imperial Defence approved the idea and the responsibility for setting up the new group was given to Captain Vernon Kell, a young army officer who spoke several languages.

At first this military intelligence organisation was known as MO5, but this was later changed to MI5, the name under which it became famous. Great efforts were made in the early days of its existence to ensure that no publicity was given to the spy catchers.

The powers of MI5 were not clearly defined in the beginning. Until 1911, for example, it was not even an offence to engage in espionage in peacetime England. Steps were taken to alter this, and later the organisation came under the Home Office for purposes of administration.

The need for a spy-hunting service was soon seen. For more than ten years before the outbreak of war in 1914 a group of German spies were living quietly in England. A senior member of the German naval intelligence service, Steinhauer, was responsible for the establishment of this network of agents.

Steinhauer made frequent visits to Great Britain, at least once as a member of the staff of the German ruler, the Kaiser. He even went as far as Scapa Flow in Scotland to check on its potential as a harbour. He took particular care to place his agents in naval ports and dockyards.

One agent, a German named Frederick Schroeder, was for eleven years the landlord of a public house near Chatham. Another, a gunner in the British navy, sold the Germans a great deal of information about the latest battleships over a two-year period. The gunner, George Parrot, was one of the first spies to be arrested with the aid of MI5. He was sentenced to four years' imprisonment.

Soon, however, an even greater feat was to be performed by Vernon Kell and his operatives. Working in conjunction with Superintendent Quinn, the head of

35 (*Right*) News media: When the news of the relief of Mafeking reached London, people were delirious with joy. The news was announced in great headlines in the newspapers. Thousands of people jammed the streets, shouting and singing. Newsboys like the one shown here distributed newspapers containing the good news free of charge. Theatrical performances were interrupted with the news, and audiences burst into 'God Save the Queen'; **36** (*Below*) An early example of the uses of technology to fight crime occurred in 1910. Dr Crippen had murdered his wife and was fleeing to Canada on a liner. He took with him Ethel Le Neve, dressed up as a boy. The captain of the ship became suspicious and sent a wireless message to London. The authorities sent a detective on a faster ship to arrest the pair. Crippen was later executed for the murder of his wife. Ethel Le Neve was acquitted. This was the first use of radio in combating crime

Scotland Yard's Special Branch, they unearthed a vital centre of German espionage in Britain.

Quinn's men had been following a suspected German agent. The man led them to a hairdresser's shop in the Caledonian Road near King's Cross in London. The shop was owned by Karl Gustav Ernst, who had been born in Britain of German parents. His shop was a cover for a secret intelligence organisation and was being used by the Germans as a 'post office'. All letters passing through Britain to and from German agents were being passed on by Ernst.

When Vernon Kell was informed of this he received permission to intercept and open all letters addressed to the hairdresser and all those leaving the shop. In this way MI5 learnt the whereabouts of practically every German agent in Great Britain. Kell did not move in on Ernst but continued to read the letters being sent to the unsuspecting hairdresser. When the war broke out, however, MI5 agents were able to arrest almost every German spy in Britain.

Alfred Redl

One of the best secret service agents in the decades just before the First World War was Alfred Redl, the head of the Austrian intelligence service. Redl made great use of the new mechanical inventions being made. For secret service purposes he adapted cameras, phonographs, the telegraph, and so on.

Unfortunately, Redl, a man of great charm, was also unscrupulous. He accepted money from the Russians to betray his country and pass on the secrets of his organisation to them. For a period of almost ten years the Austrian did just that, making a great deal of money in the process. Ignorant of what was going on, the Austrian authorities continued to think highly of their secret service chief. They even promoted him to a higher position. But this was to prove Redl's undoing.

The Austrian's successor as head of the intelligence service was Captain Maximilian Ronge. Ronge had received much of his training from Redl and was an expert at counter-espionage. After a while some of his agents reported that money was being sent regularly from Russia to Redl. At first Ronge could hardly believe that his former superior could be engaged in a cold-blooded and systematic betrayal of his country. Nevertheless he gave instructions that Redl was to be

placed under constant observation. As a result of this surveillance Redl was caught in the possession of incriminating documents. Rather than suffer the disgrace of a public trial Redl shot himself.

Outbreak of War

During the First World War the internal security of Great Britain was looked after by three organisations: MI5; the Special Branch of Scotland Yard under Sir Basil Thomson; and Naval Intelligence presided over by Sir Reginald Hall. Kell's MI5 had already broken the existing spy network and in 1914 the Germans had to set to work to train and dispatch new agents to Great Britain. Few of them had any success.

The first spy to be shot after the outbreak of war was Karl Lody, a brave but inefficient and unlucky agent. Before the war Lody had been working in the United States. He hurried home to Germany to volunteer his services. Because he spoke English fluently he was recruited and trained as a spy.

In 1914 Lody was smuggled over to England with a crowd of refugees. He bore a stolen passport and picked up a bicycle which was waiting for him. Almost at once Lody gave himself away. From Edinburgh he sent a telegram to a pre-arranged contact in Stockholm, Adolf Burchard. Unfortunately for Lody, MI5 knew that Burchard was an enemy agent. All communications addressed to him from England were being intercepted and opened.

Although Lody had received a brief training in all the modern spying aids, including the use of radio and cyphers, he made no effort to use a code when communicating with Stockholm. To MI5 it was plain that they had another spy at their mercy.

Lody was not arrested at once. Instead a military intelligence agent, posing as a journalist, struck up a friendship with the spy and accompanied him all over the country, pretending to be gathering stories for his newspaper. The intelligence agent fed the unsuspecting Lody with all manner of false information to be sent

37 Sir Basil Thomson, head of the Special Branch at Scotland Yard during the First World War, had an interesting life. The son of an Archbishop, he had been Prime Minister of Tonga in the South Pacific and Governor of Dartmoor Prison before he took up his counter-espionage duties. He interrogated Mata Hari (page 64) and tried to persuade her to abandon espionage, but she would not listen to him

back to Germany, including the erroneous report that thousands of Russian troops were passing through England on their way to the continent.

Lody proved to be a dogged and courageous agent. In the height of an air raid on London he calmly moved about the streets, ignoring the bombs and anti-aircraft guns, noting the position of the guns and seeing how much damage was being done by the bombs.

Eventually MI5 decided that it was time to move in. Lody suspected that he was being followed and tried to flee to the safety of neutral Ireland. When he was apprehended he pretended to be an American tourist, producing his stolen passport in evidence. It was of no avail. When he was searched almost £200 in various currencies was found on him, together with a notebook containing details of a recent naval battle in the North Sea and copies of his incriminating letters to Stockholm.

Lody was tried, found guilty of espionage and sentenced to be shot as a spy. The sentence was carried out within the walls of the Tower of London, traditionally the place of execution for spies and traitors. Before he faced the firing squad, Lody turned to the officer in charge of the execution.

'I suppose you won't shake hands with a spy?' he asked.

'I'll shake hands with a brave man' was the answer.

Because Kell had destroyed the original German espionage organisation, spies sent over to Great Britain constantly had to start from scratch; there were few if any other agents in the country to help them. Most spies could not overcome this handicap and eventually gave themselves away.

Two Dutchmen were sent by the German intelligence service to report on the number of British warships in Portsmouth harbour. They pretended to be cigar merchants and sent back orders for cigars to neutral Holland. In reality these orders masked a code in which details of the vessels at Portsmouth were sent on to Germany. Five thousand Havana cigars, for example, meant that five cruisers were at anchor, and so on. An alert post-office official, however, noticed that in the course of a single month the two Dutchmen seemed to be ordering more cigars than the citizens of Portsmouth could possibly smoke in a year. He informed the authorities and the spies were duly watched and then arrested.

Not all spies were as inefficient as this, but of all the agents sent to Britain during the First World War, only a handful escaped detection. One of these, Jules Silber, actually obtained a job in the postal censorship department in England and was able to send valuable information back to Germany.

Another, Trebitsch Lincoln, tried without success to be a double agent. Lincoln, born in Hungary, had made quite a career for himself in England, even becoming a Member of Parliament. He volunteered to become a spy for the British and was sent to Holland.

As soon as he reached Holland, Lincoln contacted the Germans and offered to spy for them as well. The Germans distrusted Lincoln and refused his offer. The British, suspecting what was happening, withdrew Lincoln and sent him off to the United States. When he got to America the former MP showed his hatred for his adopted country by writing a series of anti-British newspaper articles.

Sir Roger Casement

The most celebrated treason trial held in Great Britain during the war was that of Sir Roger Casement. Casement, an Irishman, had had a distinguished career as a diplomat and in 1911 had been knighted. He was also an Irish patriot who felt that Ireland should be independent of England.

Many other Irishmen were of the same opinion and on 26 April 1916, there was the celebrated **Easter Rising** in Dublin, the Irish capital. After a week of sporadic fighting the uprising was quelled by British troops. The Germans did as much as they could to encourage the Irish revolt. They hoped to use Casement as one of their principal agents in the affair. However, things went wrong almost from the start.

Soon after the beginning of the war, Casement, who had left the Foreign Service, went to Germany to make sure that the Germans would give Ireland independence if they won the war. Many Irishmen were fighting for England in the war, and some of them had been taken prisoner. Casement went to see these Irish prisoners in order to try and persuade them to form an Irish Brigade to fight against the English if necessary in the quest for Irish independence. Before Casement could complete this task, he heard of the proposed Easter Rising. He thought that such a revolt would have little chance of success and he wanted to get back to Ireland to see what he could do about it.

The Germans promised to send 20,000 rifles and plenty of ammunition to help the revolt. Casement insisted on going to Ireland with the consignment. He made the journey in a German submarine. He was dreadfully sea-sick on the way and to make matters worse, when the U-boat reached the coast of Ireland it could not make contact with the trawler carrying the guns and ammunition.

Nevertheless Casement decided to go ashore. With two companions he left the submarine in a small dinghy. The dinghy overturned but the three men managed to scramble ashore. Casement collapsed on the beach. He was too exhausted to continue so his companions left in search of some form of transport. Casement was

38 When he was a British consular official, Sir Roger Casement became well known for condemning the atrocious conditions of rubber workers in the Belgian Congo. In 1916, he came ashore from a German submarine to lead the Sinn Fein rebellion against the English, but was captured almost at once and later executed for treason

then discovered by a police constable. Refusing to believe the former's claim that he was an author out for a stroll in the small hours of the morning, the policeman arrested Casement and took him into custody.

He was transported from Dublin to London where he was interrogated by Sir Basil Thomson of the Special Branch and Sir Reginald Hall of Naval Intelligence. Casement admitted his identity. He was taken first to Brixton prison and then the Tower of London. In June 1916 he was brought to trial on a charge of treason. Witnesses were found to declare that Casement had toured German prisoner-of-war camps trying to persuade Irishmen to join the Volunteer Brigade. Casement denied that he had received money from the Germans: 'I never asked for nor accepted a single penny of foreign money, neither for myself nor for any Irish cause', he affirmed.

The jury found the Irishman guilty of high treason and he was executed at Pentonville gaol on 3 August 1916.

Mata Hari

Many tales and legends have grown up around the figure of Mata Hari, the beautiful woman spy. Most of them have been wildly exaggerated. But there was a Mata Hari and she was an agent of sorts, although neither a very good nor an enthusiastic one. Her story is really one of pathos and tragedy rather than of high adventure.

Margaretha Zelle, to give Mata Hari her real name, was born in Holland in 1876. She married an army officer some years her senior and the pair of them went to live in Java in the East Indies. The marriage was not a happy one and in 1904 she left her husband.

In an effort to earn a living Margaretha became a professional dancer. She adopted the name of Mata Hari, which is Malayan for 'eye of the day'. Mata Hari was an attractive dancer, and pretending to come from the mysterious East she made a fair living from her performances.

Her work took her to many countries, even after the outbreak of war in 1914. Early in the war she agreed to become a spy for the Germans. She was not interested in politics and had no particular liking for Germany. However, she had to earn a living and the Germans could have prevented her from dancing.

Mata Hari's career as an espionage agent was confused. She made her way to Holland and sought permission to go to England. The British suspected her intentions and refused to allow her to enter their country. After some hesitation the French intelligence service, the Deuxième Bureau, approached Mata Hari and asked her to spy for them. The woman was probably amazed at being so much in demand as an agent. Anyway she asked the French for a million francs as her fee. To her surprise, the French agreed.

Mata Hari then set out for Belgium by a roundabout sea route. On the way the vessel in which she was travelling was stopped and searched by British ships. Mata Hari was suspected of being a German spy called Clara Bendix. She was

39 Mata Hari seen in her famous Eastern dancing costume. Her real name was Margaretha Gertrude Zelle, and she was born in Holland, not the mysterious East. As a spy she was not particularly successful, and only the incompetence of the counter-espionage services in the areas where she worked led to her surviving as long as she did. Mata Hari was executed by a firing squad in Paris in 1917

taken off the ship and escorted to London.

In England she was interviewed by Sir Basil Thomson of the Special Branch. She told him that she was spying for the French, Britain's allies. The Deuxième Bureau, for reasons best known to the French, denied all knowledge of the woman. Thomson did not know what to believe. The French may have been lying. On the other hand this attractive dancer might be a German spy. In the end Thomson sent Mata Hari to neutral Spain. It is possible that the British, too, asked her to spy for them. It must have been a bewildering experience for her.

Once she had settled in Spain she posed as a British dancer, Lady Macleod. She also befriended a number of Germans, including the head of their intelligence service in Madrid. In addition she maintained contact with the French. By this time nobody was sure who Mata Hari was working for; sometimes she must have wondered herself. Foolishly she returned to France. She was arrested and tried as a spy.

At her trial Mata Hari claimed that she had been friendly with the Germans only to obtain information for the French. She also pointed out that as a citizen of neutral Holland she owed no loyalty to any of the participants in the war. In the end Mata Hari was sentenced to death. The sentence was carried out on 15 October 1917.

British agents

British agents in Germany were much more successful, on the whole, than their

German counterparts had been in England. British military commanders, like those of Germany, realised many years before the outbreak of war that hostilities between the two countries were almost inevitable. Many of them were also of the opinion that a thorough knowledge of the future movements of the German army would be of the greatest assistance.

A leading British general was Henry Wilson. Wilson was convinced that a war with England and France on the one hand against Germany on the other would some day come about. He made every effort to talk to the French military leaders and did all that he could to foster co-operation between the two armies.

Three or four times a year Wilson would travel by motor car and bicycle along the borders between France and Germany and France and Belgium, learning as much as he could about the lie of the land over which he was sure invading German forces would one day pour. He made detailed notes about areas which he thought were potential battlefields.

When Wilson went back to the War Office in London he constructed an enormous map of Belgium covering an entire wall. On this map he marked in all the roads likely to be used by the Germans in their advance when the war finally broke out. Thanks to Wilson and some of the French generals, when the war did begin the Allies had prepared an effective battle plan.

They had also planted spies in Germany and in most other European countries, whose only function was to wait quietly until the outbreak of war before attempting to transmit information. Great Britain alone had over forty spies or groups of spies waiting in Germany by 1914, and few of them were caught. So successful were most of these agents that to this day the full effectiveness of the British espionage system in Germany in the First World War is not known.

One so-called British agent who received a great deal of publicity was not a spy at all. Her name was Edith Cavell, and she was a British nurse who for some years had been living in Brussels, the capital of Belgium. Belgium had been overrun by the German forces and a great many British and French troops had been cut off from their units and were trying to escape over the border to neutral Holland.

Some of them found their way to Edith Cavell. She sheltered the soldiers, gave them food and money and sent them on their way to the border. The Germans found out what was happening. They arrested Edith Cavell and tried her on charges of recruiting soldiers and spying for the Allies. She denied both charges, saying that her only crime had been to help men escape over the frontier.

Edith Cavell was found guilty of aiding war prisoners to escape. She was sentenced to death and executed before a firing squad in October 1916. Her death caused a storm of protest throughout the world.

A woman who was a genuine agent for the British during the First World War was Marthe Cnockaert, who was born in Belgium. When her country was occupied by the Germans she was forced into service as a nurse at a military hospital. In a short time she had been recruited as an agent by British Intelligence. For two years this courageous and resourceful woman who worked behind the enemy lines was in constant danger of discovery and execution, but she kept the British fully informed of German troop movements. Not all her warnings were heeded. News of a major German gas attack was ignored and many Allied troops were badly gassed.

Marthe even helped to blow up a German supply dump. In carrying this out, however, she lost her wrist watch. It was found by the Germans and the owner was identified. Marthe was arrested and tried as a spy. She was found guilty and sentenced to death. The sentence was later changed to one of life imprisonment. She had served two years of this when the war ended. Marthe was released at once and was decorated for her heroism by the Allied governments.

Lawrence of Arabia

One of the best known and most glamorous of all British agents in the First World War was the almost legendary Colonel T. E. Lawrence, better known as Lawrence of Arabia. Some of his exploits were almost certainly exaggerated, but even so his conduct in the war in the Middle East resembled more the hero of a novel than that of an espionage agent.

Soon after the outbreak of war Lawrence, a quiet, withdrawn man, was attached to an Intelligence section working in Cairo. The British were fighting the Turks, the allies of the Germans in this part of the world. Lawrence heard that the Emir Feisal, an Arab leader, was endeavouring to fight the Turks in the desert.

Dressed as an Arab, a costume he was to retain for most of the war, Lawrence went to meet Feisal. The two men took to each other and Lawrence, acting as an official British agent, persuaded the Arab chieftain to reorganise his army and attack a vital railway line.

It was the start of ferocious fighting in the desert. Lawrence in his Arab costume seemed to be everywhere, urging, encouraging and organising. He raised the northern tribes to fight against the Turks. He raided behind the Turkish lines. After a bloody battle at Maan he forced a passage to the sea.

The Turks had to divert large numbers of their men from fighting the British in order to face this new threat from Lawrence and his Arabs. The British military leaders in the area realised how effective these sudden raids by the Arabs were. They supplied Lawrence with weapons and large sums of money. For the rest of the war he continued to swoop on the Turks. One attempt to cut a vital railway line only just failed. Then in 1918 when the Turks finally fell back Lawrence and his Arabs entered the city of Damascus in triumph, ahead of the main British force.

After the war Lawrence failed to settle down to civilian life. For a while he was a research scholar at Oxford University and then an adviser to the Colonial Office. During this period he saw his old comrade in arms, Feisal, become a king. In 1922 Lawrence abandoned everything and enlisted as a mechanic in the airforce. A year later he left and became a private soldier in the tank corps, only to transfer back to the airforce in 1925. Ten years later he left the RAF altogether and in that same year was killed in a motor-cycle accident.

40 (*Right*) T E Lawrence is seen here talking to some Arab leaders during the First World War. Lawrence first went to the Middle East as a junior member of an archaeological team sent by the British Museum. During the war he emerged as a dashing leader of the Arabs who owed allegiance to Emir Feisal. He conducted many daring raids on Turkish positions in the desert. After the war he became disillusioned and withdrew from public life. He enlisted in the army and twice in the RAF. He was killed in a road accident in 1935

41 (*Below*) British counter-espionage was efficient during the First World War and few enemy agents survived for long. In Britain, most German agents were rounded up as soon as the war began. In France, nearer the front line, German agents had some success in signalling at night to their own troops. This illustration shows two agents being caught in the act of passing on information

Other agents

One of the most influential of the agents who worked in the First World War was the Russian, Parvus. Parvus was one of the small band of Russians who conspired to overthrow the Tsar and bring the war to an end. By 1917 the Russian people had had enough of both the war and the rule of the Russian emperors. More and more Russians were willing to follow the Bolshevik socialists under Lenin and his companions, overthrow the Tsar and bring the war to an end.

The Germans were delighted at the prospect of one of the nations ranged against them leaving the war altogether. They did all that they could to support and encourage the Bolsheviks. Parvus was the man chosen to negotiate secretly with the Germans.

As early as 1915 Parvus was negotiating in Berlin. The Germans gave him a passport and allocated the sum of two million marks to be spent on helping the Russian Revolution. Parvus travelled all over Europe, meeting some of the exiled revolutionaries and making plans for the revolution, especially for the part to be played in it by the Germans. When the revolution finally took place in 1917, the Tsar was overthrown with very little trouble and Russia withdrew from the war.

Further Reading——
Borer, *The First World War* (Macmillan).
O'Connor, *The Russian Revolution* (Heinemann).
Mack, *Lenin and the Russian Revolution* (Longman).
Pelling, *Modern Britain* (Nelson).

8 Spies in Peacetime

The conclusion of the First World War did not bring with it an end to suspicion and hostility between nations or between groups and classes of people within nations. The 21 uneasy years of peace after 1918 were full of intrigue.

The espionage and counter-espionage services of Great Britain were starved of funds in the period between the wars, but they did not lack work. At various times there were bitter clashes between the authorities and the Irish, the Communists, the Fascists and the trade unions. In all cases the counter-espionage services of MI5 and the Special Branch were involved.

The Irish and the Communists

By the end of the war many of the Irish were adamant in their demands for com-

42 On 26 April 1916 the Irish rose in Dublin. Fighting against the English troops lasted for a week during this celebrated Easter Rising. A number of buildings were destroyed, including these ones in Sackville Street, before the revolt was put down

plete independence from England. Failing to achieve this they embarked upon a desperate struggle. There were riots, ambushes and assassinations.

The British secret service was not very successful during the Irish struggle. This was partly due to the fact that there was considerable confusion between the British army in Ireland and the organisation known as the Black and Tans, consisting of former servicemen who had been recruited to help keep order in Ireland. Instead of helping each other the two groups were often hostile. The Black and Tans often dispensed with the orthodox secret service and used their own agents and paid informers. Prices were put on the heads of rebel leaders, and sometimes these fugitives were betrayed for the money.

A few British agents penetrated the ranks of the Sinn Fein and the Irish Republican Army, but they failed to bring back information of much use. The Irish were much more successful in their attempts at espionage. When one of their leaders, Eamon de Valera, was arrested and imprisoned, his comrades promptly rescued him. Another Irish leader, Michael Collins, planted his spies in both the police force and the ranks of the British army, before he was murdered.

The Irish were engaged in a form of guerrilla warfare, and they succeeded in most of their aims. In 1922 the Irish Free State was formed, separate from Northern Ireland, and in 1937 this became the independent nation of Eire.

While the agents of MI5 and the Special Branch were busy in Ireland, there were also many calls upon their services in England, especially to combat widespread fears of the Communists. After the Russian Revolution the Communists has assumed control of the country and Communist parties were being formed in other European countries, including Great Britain.

Some people even feared a Communist revolution in Great Britain. It was a period of what were known as 'red scares', when people began to suspect Communists of all sorts of evil intentions. This was allied to a great deal of industrial unrest caused by poor wages and working conditions and widespread unemployment. There was considerable ill-feeling in the country.

Affairs were not helped by what became known as the Zinoviev Letter. In 1924, several newspapers published the text of a letter which was supposed to have been sent to the British Communist party by Zinoviev, one of the Russian leaders. The letter declared that the British Communists should do all within their power to stir up general unrest, because 'it is indispensable to stir up the masses of the British proletariat'.

The letter, published just before a general election, caused consternation in the country. People thought that Britain might be on the point of revolution. The Socialist party, which was in power, suffered considerably because voters thought that Socialists were sympathetic towards the Russians. The Socialists were defeated and the Conservative party gained power.

Afterwards it was suspected that the letter was a forgery, concocted by enemies of Russia. It was established that the Conservative party had paid £5,000 for the letter and had given it to newspapers in order that the Socialists should gain bad publicity just before the election.

Sidney Reilly

A freelance agent and former spy who was suspected of having a hand in circulating the Zinoviev Letter was Sidney Reilly. Reilly was a reckless, highly-intelligent man, born of Russian parents, who spent most of his life as a spy for one power or another. In 1900 he was spying for the Japanese in Manchuria. He was betrayed and only just escaped with his life to Russia. There he was recruited as an agent for the British secret service, and in the First World War he worked as a spy in Germany.

Some of the more flamboyant agents like Reilly were not above exaggerating the details of their exploits. Even so, Sidney Reilly does appear to have carried out some amazing feats. In the first place he was parachuted into Germany, at a time when military aviation was virtually in its infancy and parachutes were far from safe. Once he was in the country he actually joined the German army for a time. On another occasion he stole the uniform of a high-ranking officer and attended a secret conference.

Towards the end of the war Reilly was withdrawn from Germany and sent on several journeys to Russia. His brief was to prevent the Russians withdrawing from the war, but he could not persuade Lenin and his colleagues to keep up the struggle. In Russia Reilly joined two other British agents, Paul Dukes and Bruce Lockhart, but even although he managed to obtain a position as an official in the ranks of the Bolsheviks he could not influence events. Eventually he fell under suspicion and had to flee the country.

After the war Reilly continued his work as an agent. He was engaged in the conspiracy to circulate the Zinoviev Letter, and then returned to Russia, again as a spy. This time his good fortune deserted him. He was arrested, tried and shot.

The trade unions and the Fascists

Two other organisations which caused MI5 and the Special Branch great concern were the trade unions and the British Union of Fascists. The trade unions had been growing in power and were increasingly distressed about the economic state of the country. Many workers could not find employment, especially in the mining industry; those who could find work were badly paid.

It became apparent that industrial unrest was inevitable and that the trade unions would play an important part in this. MI5 began to infiltrate agents into the different trade unions to report back on what was happening in an effort to avert disaster.

There was little that the agents could do except agree that large-scale strikes seemed inevitable. On 2 May 1926, at midnight, the General Strike began. It lasted until 12 May. Throughout the dispute agents and spies in the labour ranks kept the police and MI5 informed of what went on at most union meetings.

Agents were also planted among the ranks of the Blackshirts, as the members of

43 A familiar sight in London in the 1930s was members of the British Fascist movement selling their newspaper. The British Union of Fascists was formed by Sir Oswald Mosley. Members of his party held many meetings before the war, and there were often clashes with Communists and Jews. During the Second World War Mosley was detained in prison

44 Unrest in Britain before the Second World War was displayed in a number of ways. One of them was the celebrated 'Jarrow Crusade'. Unemployed workers from Jarrow marched to London to protest against their conditions. This demonstration is sometimes called 'The Hunger March'

the British Fascist movement were known in the period between the wars. There were pitched battles in the streets of London and other cities between Fascists and Communists and between Fascists and Jews. The authorities tried to forestall these riots by obtaining information of confrontations in advance from their agents and seeing that plenty of policemen were in position at the appropriate spots.

Individual agents

MI5 and the Special Branch had their work cut out in identifying and dealing with individual agents in Great Britain in the 1920s and 1930s. In 1923, to the considerable surprise of many, it was announced that Vernon Kell, the quiet head of MI5 was retiring. In reality this announcement was a ruse. Kell was to continue at the head of the organisation for another seventeen years. It was felt, however, that if other powers thought that the highly-respected Kell was no longer in charge of Britain's security arrangements it might lull them into a sense of false security.

The counter-espionage organisations certainly managed to arrest a number of agents in this period, but it is now generally held that MI5 went through an ineffective patch between the wars. One reason for this was that it was deprived of money. Another was that a number of major mistakes were made in recruiting personnel. It was a time when patriotism was being regarded by many as being of less importance than ideology. It did not matter what country a man belonged to, it was what he believed in that was important.

At this period many people were turning to Communism as an answer to the ills of the world. A number of the agents recruited by MI5 were secretly Communists. They kept this to themselves and over the years a number of them rose high in the service of the organisation. As time went on they were able to relay more and more important information to Russia.

Even so, one or two enemy agents were unearthed by MI5. One of the most important of these was a Communist called Percy Glading. Glading had spent a year in Russia in 1929, being trained in methods of espionage. However, he was already known to MI5 as a leader of strikes and disputes and he was carefully watched. MI5 even managed to plant an agent on Glading in the form of a young woman who was in reality an official of MI5. She became Glading's girl-friend and managed to obtain enough information about him and one of his contacts, an examiner at Woolwich Arsenal, to get them both arrested. Glading was sentenced to six years' imprisonment.

Another celebrated espionage case of the 1930s was the so-called affair of the officer in the Tower. This was a lieutenant in the British army, a man called Baillie-Stewart, who was accused of selling information to the Germans. He was arrested and detained for a while in the Tower of London before his trial. He was found guilty of espionage and sentenced in 1933 to three years' imprisonment.

At about the same period a number of British engineers working in Russia were also arrested and accused of spying for their country. They were brought to trial

45 Baillie-Stewart, with his hands over his face, arrives under escort at the Duke of York's Headquarters, Chelsea, for his trial

but the British government protested so vigorously that eventually all the engineers were allowed to come home.

MI5 and the Special Branch were not helped in the years immediately before the Second World War by a large influx of foreign refugees fleeing from persecution in Europe. The vast majority were genuine fugitives, but a number were German spies taking advantage of the confusion to enter the country.

When it became apparent that another world war was likely, Kell and his colleagues were allowed more money, but by this time it was almost too late. The espionage and counter-espionage services of the country had been allowed to run down and were in a weak state.

Further Reading——
Smith, *The Trade Unions* (Oliver and Boyd).
Hastings, *Between the Wars* (Benn).
Smith (ed), *1000 Makers of the Twentieth Century* (David and Charles).
Chester, Fay & Young, *The Zinoviev Letter* (Heinemann).
Lockhart, *Ace of Spies* (Hodder and Stoughton).

9 Spies in the Second World War

During the Second World War espionage flourished as never before, so much so that it would be impossible to do more than outline the major trends and mention some of the major personalities associated with spying between 1939 and 1945.

Perhaps the most successful spy of the entire war was a Russian, Richard Sorge, who operated in Japan before and during the war. He made friends in the highest diplomatic and military positions. He discovered in advance the dates of the proposed German attack on Russia in 1941 and the Japanese onslaught on Pearl Harbour in the following year. Eventually Sorge was discovered and executed.

Another highly successful Russian agent was Rudolph Roessler, a journalist who lived in neutral Switzerland. Somehow Roessler made contact with a highly-placed traitor on Hitler's staff. Using this source the agent provided a great deal of useful information for his masters in Moscow. In 1944 Roessler was arrested by the Swiss, but he was soon released.

German spies

At the beginning of the First World War the authorities had been able to round up practically every German spy operating in Great Britain. They were not to be so fortunate in 1939, and a number of German spies were able to work successfully against Britain throughout the war years.

Prominent among Britons who spied against their own country was a Welshman, Arthur Owens. Owens was a Welsh Nationalist who wanted independence for Wales. His business as a salesman often took him to the Continent. On one of these trips before the war he was approached by the Germans, who had heard of his anti-British sentiments. Owens agreed to spy for Germany and was able to provide information about the location of airfields. Upon the outbreak of war Owens actually visited Germany to receive fresh instructions. For the remainder of the war years he rendered valuable service to the Germans, including helping enemy agents who were parachuted into Britain.

One of the most successful of these agents was Hans Schmidt, a Dane who in 1940 was parachuted into England with another spy, Jorgen Bjornson. Both Danes were to pose as refugees while obtaining as much information as they could about British preparations for the expected German invasion.

During their parachute descent Bjornson fell into a tree, hurting his leg. Schmidt did his best to hide the injured agent and then contacted Arthur Owens in Winchester. Despite their efforts Bjornson was arrested and interned.

Schmidt was much more successful, avoiding all efforts to capture him. He had a most useful espionage career, sending back information on Allied troop movements and the position of air bases. He obtained a job on a farm and even married the farmer's daughter. At the end of the war Schmidt was still undetected.

Other spies were less successful. More than fifteen were captured, tried and executed in the war years in Britain. A number of traitors were also arrested during and after the war, including William Joyce who had broadcast propaganda for the Germans and had been given the nickname of 'Lord Haw Haw'.

Joyce claimed to have been born in the United States, but on his application for a passport he had stated that he had been born in Ireland. A number of Irishmen took advantage of the outbreak of war to press the claims of Irish independence. Under the leadership of Sean Russell, members of the Irish Republican Army engaged in a number of acts of sabotage in London and other large English cities, blowing up railway stations, sewage works and electricity and gas installations. Scotland Yard's Special Branch was hard-pressed to cope with this outbreak of violence, but the death of Russell was a severe blow to the IRA and by 1943 the organisation's efforts were tailing off.

German sympathisers and agents were also busy in other parts of the world. Perhaps the most audacious was the man given the code name of 'Cicero'. His real name was Elyesa Bazna, a Turk who had once been a professional singer. During the war he obtained a post as personal servant to the British ambassador

46 These sound locators were situated on the Sussex Downs at the beginning of the Second World War. Their function was to try and pick up the noise of approaching German aeroplanes. Once the locators had been fixed on the sound, they could give information about the position of the aircraft to anti-aircraft batteries guarding the coast

47 The British Broadcasting Corporation did much to keep up the morale of its listeners during the war. Speeches by the Prime Minister Winston Churchill had enormous audiences, as did news broadcasts. Variety shows like ITMA ('It's That Man Again') were extremely popular. Propaganda and news bulletins were also broadcast to enemy-occupied territory

in neutral Turkey. Almost at once Bazna noticed that security arrangements at the embassy were extremely lax. He made copies of secret documents and sold them to the Germans for large sums of money. Before long, while the ambassador was having his morning bath or playing the piano in the afternoon, Bazna was busily photographing all the documents he could lay his hands on.

Although the Germans accepted these photographs and continued to pay Bazna, they did not trust him, thinking he might be a double agent. Accordingly they paid little attention to the information supplied. Eventually American counter-espionage agents discovered the existence of Cicero and planted a woman as a secretary in the German embassy in Ankara. She even managed to meet the unsuspecting Bazna. However, the Germans warned their agent that he had been detected and Bazna was able to avoid trouble. The final ironic twist to the story came when Bazna discovered that for all his invaluable information he had been paid by the Germans in worthless counterfeit notes!

British spies

British espionage was conducted in many fashions and by a number of different agencies during the war. On the military and naval side frogmen and midget submarines entered enemy harbours, and small long-range units of soldiers operated behind the enemy lines in the deserts and jungles.

Sometimes these espionage expeditions developed into open warfare. An example of this occurred in 1942, when three British motor torpedo boats were ordered to carry out a patrol under the leadership of Lieutenant Gould off the coast of Tunisia in North Africa to find out whether the Germans were preparing to withdraw their troops from North Africa. The three vessels flew the German flag, hoping to deceive any enemy aircraft, and even dropped anchor in a harbour being used by the Germans. The British sailors calmly made maps of the area and prepared to return to their base. On the way back, however, they encountered two Italian mine-sweepers. Gould ordered the German flags to be lowered and British flags raised. He then attacked the enemy ships and went on to attack and destroy a German destroyer. Gould himself was killed in the action.

British agents were also located in all the neutral countries. Lisbon in Portugal was a particular hive of espionage, British and German agents both working there in large numbers.

There were even carefully-laid plans for an underground espionage organisation to be set up in Great Britain should the Germans have succeeded in occupying the country. The Allies were also helped by underground movements operating in the occupied nations of Europe. There were active groups in Poland and Holland. Agents in Norway and Denmark helped to destroy plants producing heavy water for German atomic research. In Belgium, the group known as 'Red Riding Hood' provided a great deal of information. Later in the war agents in occupied territories discovered the whereabouts of the bases launching German rockets to attack Great Britain. A number of underground organisations helped smuggle escaped Allied prisoners of war back to Great Britain or to neutral countries.

Even in Germany itself there were plots against Hitler. One attempt to kill the German leader by exploding a bomb at a meeting he was attending almost succeeded. Hitler was bruised and shaken by the explosion but otherwise unhurt. The conspirators were executed.

British Intelligence suffered a major blow as early as 1939 when two of their leading operatives in Europe, Major Stevens and Captain Best, were lured to the German frontier, kidnapped and taken into Germany. The Germans were thus able to break up a British spy ring at the outset of the war. This exploit occurred only a month after a German agent in Scotland had supplied such accurate information about the naval defences at Scapa Flow that a German U-boat had entered the harbour undetected and destroyed the battleship *Royal Oak*.

In an effort to recover from these setbacks the British set up an organisation in 1940 known as Special Operations Executive, or SOE for short. The main purpose of SOE was sabotage behind the enemy lines, and after an uncertain start its operatives succeeded very well. There were sometimes jealousies with the rival British intelligence organisations, and examples of co-operation with the underground movements of the countries being penetrated were not all that they should have been, but many brave men and women worked for SOE.

Among its women workers were Odette Sansom and Violette Szabo, who were two of the bravest and most successful, while an Indian princess, Noor Inayat Khan, also worked behind the enemy lines as a radio operator in France. Like a number of others she was betrayed, arrested and executed.

A highly unusual and ingenious espionage scheme launched by British Intelligence during the war was the project known as Operation Mincemeat. This took place in 1943. The Allies were about to invade North Africa and Sicily but wanted to make the Germans think that their attack would be launched against the South of France. Accordingly a dead body was obtained and dressed in the uniform of an officer in the Royal Marines. Specially forged 'top-secret' documents were prepared purporting to give details of a proposed invasion of France. These papers were put into a brief case chained to the wrist of the corpse.

The body and the documents were then conveyed in a submarine and put into the sea off the coast of neutral Spain. The body was washed ashore. German agents in Spain, thinking that the body was that of a British special messenger killed in an aeroplane crash in the Mediterranean, copied the misleading information and sent it to Berlin.

Another example of deception occurred when British Intelligence agents discovered that an officer in the Pay Corps bore a close resemblance to General Montgomery who was to lead the British invasion of France. In an effort to make the Germans think that Montgomery was interested in other areas than the coast of Normandy, the Pay Corps officer was disguised as the general and sent to Gibraltar and North Africa while the real Montgomery continued to help plan the D-Day landings.

Techniques

It was in the Second World War that the techniques and equipment of espionage were really developed. All nations involved in the war had their training schools for agents, and a variety of equipment was evolved to help agents in their work. Maps were printed on silk so that they could be folded away and not rustle. A variety of compasses were devised, including one which consisted of a tiny steel bar. When dangled from a thread, one end of the bar, specially treated, always pointed to the north. Razor blades were magnetized so that they too could be used as compasses. A cigarette-holder was invented which, when unscrewed, revealed a miniature telescope. Tiny radio receivers and transmitters were concealed in cigarette packets. A variety of lethal firearms were developed, and one weapon consisted of a fountain pen which fired darts.

Agents were also schooled in the use of codes and cyphers so that they could send information back with as little trouble as possible. Some of these codes and cyphers were extremely clever and defied detection. A code consists of secret messages where both sender and recipient possess the same codebook. Should the codebook fall into enemy hands, as happened in the First World War when the German naval codebook was acquired by the Allies, then messages using this code can

48 Tyler Kent with his mother. Kent was a clerk in the American Embassy until 1940 when he was convicted for the theft of secret diplomatic documents which he turned over to the Germans. He was sentenced to seven years' imprisonment, but was released after serving only five, and was deported

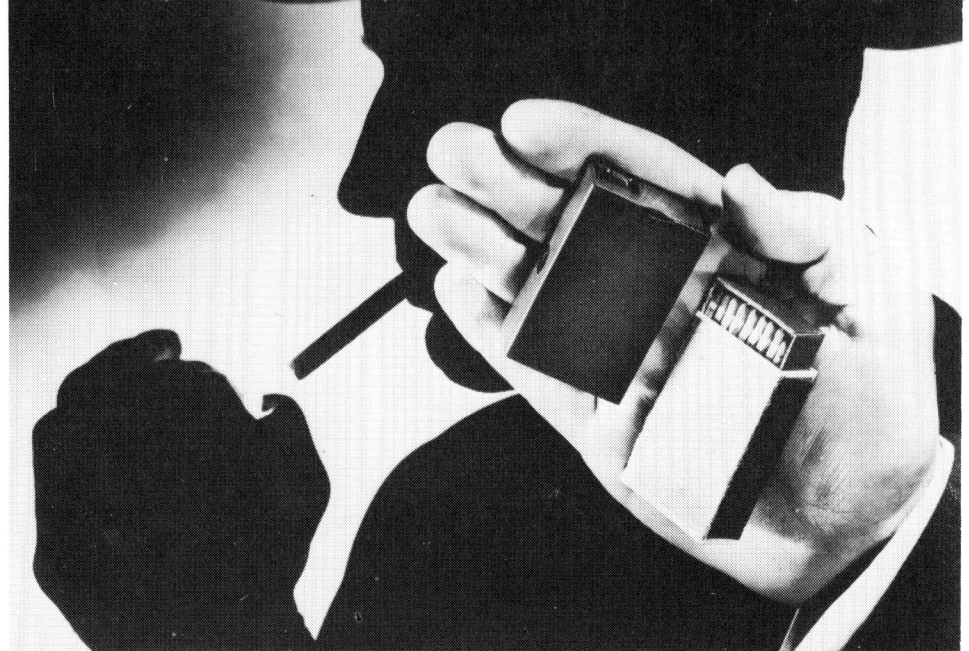

49 By the end of the Second World War, many ingenious technical devices had been manufactured to help secret agents in their work. This secret camera, held against a matchbox to show its size, could take pictures about half-an-inch square. A thousand such cameras were in use during the war

easily be deciphered. Cyphers are messages where the letters used can be changed into other letters: for example if the letter *e* is used then the recipient may know that the letter *i* is meant. Cyphers can be broken down by experts. This happened at the beginning of the Second World War when a Japanese cypher was solved by American specialists.

Other Agencies

By the end of the war intelligence agencies were proliferating. In Great Britain in addition to MI5, MI6 and the Special Branch, there were the Political Warfare Executive, Naval Intelligence, various propaganda organisations and many other smaller secret service departments and groups. In America the Central Intelligence Agency was responsible for considerable espionage activity.

Further Reading——
Peacock, *The Second World War* (Macmillan).
Manvell, *The Conspirators* (Ballantine).
West, *The Meaning of Treason* (Macmillan).
Farago, *War of Wits* (Hutchinson).

The post-war years saw some aspects of espionage reaching new peaks of professionalism as far as the development of equipment and techniques were concerned. They also introduced an increasing number of acts of espionage committed by deeply concerned men who felt that patriotism, as Nurse Cavell had said, was not enough. They believed that no country should have a monopoly of information and expertise, but that these things should be shared for the benefit of all countries and all men.

Sometimes these two types of agent, the amateur and the professional, worked apart, but occasionally they collaborated on a project, and when they did the results were often tragic and confusing. During this period there were also equally sad examples of error and incompetence of the sort which seem inevitably associated with the history of espionage.

The nuclear spies

The Second World War had ended with the explosion of two atomic bombs at Hiroshima and Nagasaki in Japan. Russia, however, had not been involved in the Allied experiments which had led to the development of nuclear weapons and was some years behind Great Britain and the USA in this respect.

With the growing mistrust between Russia and her satellite countries on one hand and the Western Allies on the other, the Russians were desperately concerned to bring themselves up-to-date in nuclear research. They pressed all kinds of agents into use—active professionals; spies planted years before and never used; and troubled and bewildered scientists uncertain of their allegiance.

The scope of the Russian efforts began to come to light as early as 1945. In this year Igor Gouzenko, an obscure Russian cypher clerk working in the Russian embassy in Ottawa, decided to defect. He liked living in Canada and reasoned that if he stole enough important documents from the embassy, he could give them to the Canadian authorities in return for permission to stay in the country.

Gouzenko found the first part of his plan easy enough to carry out. He simply went to an embassy safe and stole a handful of documents. The second part was much more difficult. To his amazement and increasing horror he could find no-one in Ottawa prepared to take the documents from him.

Gouzenko and his precious documents were turned away in succession by a newspaper, the police and the staff of the Canadian Prime Minister, all of whom he approached in order to get someone to listen to his story.

The bewildered would-be defector and his papers were saved, ironically enough, by the Russians themselves. When they discovered that the documents and the

50 This is part of the headquarters of the International Nuclear Information Service. It began operations in 1970. It has catalogued some 85,000 publications concerning the peaceful use of the atom. It enables scientists and researchers everywhere to keep in touch with nuclear developments. An organisation of this sort was probably what Alan Nunn May wanted before he began to give away nuclear secrets

clerk were missing, agents were sent round to Gouzenko's flat and broke into it. Fortunately Gouzenko was away. A neighbour, already alerted by the cypher clerk, heard the noise of the hurried search and sent for the police.

At last the authorities began to believe that there might be something to the Russian's tale. Belatedly they studied the documents he had been trying to force upon them. To their amazement they discovered that the papers gave details of a Russian spy-ring in North America which had already stolen atomic secrets.

These documents led to the discovery of a number of agents and traitors, all of whom were watched and in some cases implicated other agents. The first man to be arrested was Alan Nunn May, a British scientist. After a brilliant career as a student and university lecturer, which included a visit to Russia in 1936, May had worked on atomic research in Canada during the war. He had been upset because the Russians were not kept informed of progress and in 1945 began passing on information to Moscow.

When May's name was seen among the documents stolen by Gouzenko, the scientist was watched and arrested in London in 1946. He was sentenced to 10 years' imprisonment. Many of his fellow-scientists protested that May had been right in principle and that no nation had the right to keep scientific discoveries to itself.

Another physicist arrested as a result of the Ottawa incident was Klaus Fuchs, a German refugee who joined the British team working on atomic research during the war. Unlike May, who had given away secrets because of his belief in the unity of man, Fuchs was a Communist and almost from the beginning was sending carbons of his research to the Russian embassy in London. Sent to the USA to carry on his research he continued to pass on information to the Russians through one of their agents, an American Communist called Harry Gold.

Although he was closely watched, Fuchs was not arrested until 1950. By this time he had become disenchanted with the Russians and was close to a nervous breakdown. At his trial he pleaded guilty and was sentenced to 14 years' imprisonment.

In the USA, Harry Gold, the spy Fuchs had contacted, was also arrested. He was sentenced to 30 years' imprisonment, and during his trial implicated another agent hired by the Russians, David Greenglass, a young technician at the Los Alamos research centre.

In his turn Greenglass named his sister and brother-in-law, Ethel and Julius Rosenberg, as being Russian agents. They had both joined the Communist party in the USA in the 1930s and had acted as undercover agents for the Russians during the war. When Ethel's brother had obtained work in a minor technical capacity at Los Alamos, the Rosenbergs put great pressure on him to tell them as much as possible about the construction of the place. This he reluctantly did.

The arrest of the Rosenbergs coincided with a great wave of anti-Communist feeling in the USA where people were horrified at the rate at which secret information seemed to be getting to Russia. Their trial was highly publicised and great controversy was aroused when the Rosenbergs were sentenced to death and executed.

The professionals
The defection of a cypher clerk and the subsequent series of arrests in Great Britain and the USA as a result of the documents provided by Gouzenko had provided a succession of shattering blows for the Soviet secret service overseas.

51 The tombstone on the left was used as a 'letter box' by a spy. It is in a corner of St Mary's Churchyard in Portsmouth. Siroj Abdool Cager, a clerk for the Greater London Council, passed on the names of the owners of diplomatic cars to Oleg Lyalin, a Russian agent. Cager would leave his messages in pre-arranged places like this tombstone, to be retrieved later by the Russians. Cager was caught and sentenced to three years' imprisonment

Promptly the Russians set out to rebuild their organisation. Much of the work in the Western world was entrusted to one man—Colonel Rudolf Abel.

Abel was an excellent professional spy. He was intelligent, courageous, resourceful and experienced. During the war he had worked in German occupied Russia and had also done outstanding intelligence work in the Middle East. After the war he had operated in France and Germany before being sent to rebuild the Russian spy network in the United States.

In 1948 Abel set himself up as a photographer in New York. Hidden in his studio was a powerful short-wave radio set. His assistant was another extremely talented and dedicated professional spy who went under the name of Gordon Lonsdale. Lonsdale worked for three years under Abel before being sent to head a spy ring in Great Britain.

Abel and Lonsdale had done a great deal to rebuild the shattered Soviet espionage service in North America. Unfortunately Lonsdale's replacement proved a disaster. He was a man called Huyhanen, a most inefficient operative. Abel complained about Huyhanen to his superiors in Moscow. His assistant heard of this and feared the consequences. In 1957 he fled to the American embassy in Paris, betraying Abel. Once again the Soviet spy-ring in North America had been given away by a defector.

Abel was arrested in New York and brought to trial. He was convicted of espionage. Initially he was sentenced to death but this was later changed to 30 years' imprisonment. Abel served only a few years before being exchanged for an American spy captured by the Russians. Espionage agencies always did their best to look after their operatives and secure their release should they be caught.

Burgess, Maclean and the Third Man

In 1950, there was considerable disturbance in Great Britain when a British citizen, Bruno Pontecorvo, a scientist engaged upon atomic weapons research, fled to Russia and began to work on nuclear research there. The reasons for his defection were never fully explained.

There was an even greater uproar in the following year when it was announced that two British diplomats had disappeared. Later the government admitted with reluctance that the two men had defected to the Russians. The diplomats were Donald Maclean and Guy Burgess. Their defection stunned their friends and colleagues. Both men, although eccentric and known to be heavy drinkers, had been considered completely loyal. The fact that two diplomats could go over to another power, apparently for ideological reasons or matters of conscience, was a significant event in the history of modern espionage.

Donald Maclean was born in 1913, the son of a successful politician. He went to a good school and then to Cambridge University. Guy Burgess was at the university at the same time. Both men became Communists. It was a time, in the 1930s, when many young men, dissatisfied with their own governments' attempts to solve the problems of the world, joined the Communist party in the hope that

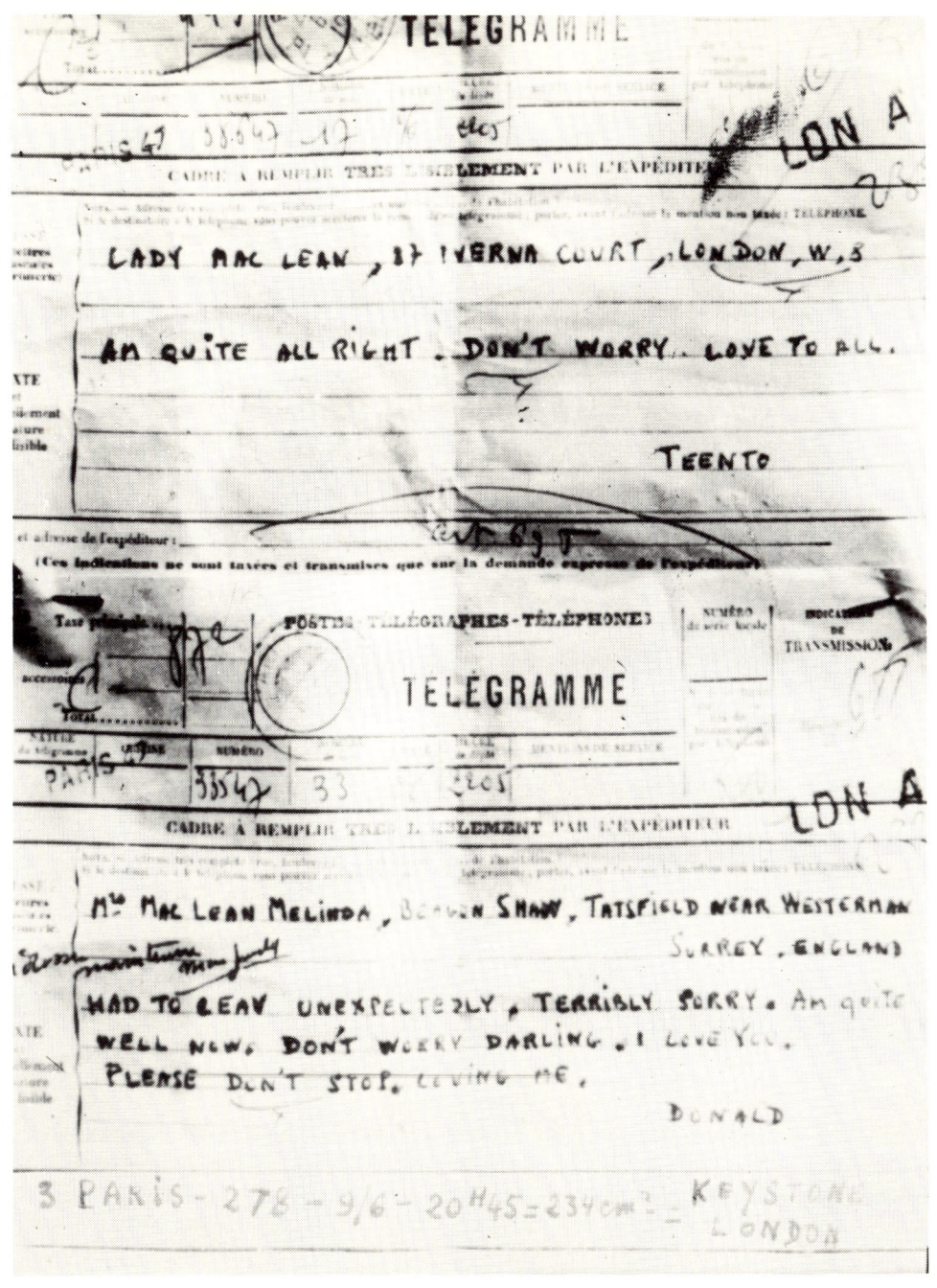

LADY MAC LEAN, 37 IVERNA COURT, LONDON, W.8

AM QUITE ALL RIGHT. DON'T WORRY. LOVE TO ALL.

TEENTO

Mrs MAC LEAN MELINDA, BEACON SHAW, TATSFIELD NEAR WESTERHAM
SURREY, ENGLAND

HAD TO LEAV UNEXPECTEDLY, TERRIBLY SORRY. AM QUITE
WELL NOW, DON'T WORRY DARLING. I LOVE YOU.
PLEASE DON'T STOP, LOVING ME.

DONALD

52 Telegrams sent from Donald Maclean to his mother and his wife. These telegrams confirmed that Maclean had fled the country. A great uproar followed and the British security authorities were severely criticised for allowing Maclean and Guy Burgess to escape

this philosophy would succeed where others seemed to be failing.

Donald Maclean left Cambridge in 1935 to work in the Foreign Office, serving in London and Paris. In 1944 he was sent to the British embassy in Washington. It was here that he was probably approached by the Russians, who knew of his political sympathies. He began to supply them with secret information. In 1948, Maclean was transferred to Egypt. By this time he was drinking heavily and engaging in brawls. He was sent back to London for a rest and medical treatment.

Burgess, who fled to Moscow at the same time as Maclean, was another heavy drinker. He too had served in the Washington embassy and had been sent home in disgrace. The authorities were beginning to suspect the two men of being traitors. Before they could move in Burgess and Maclean escaped to Russia. When it was finally admitted that both men had almost certainly been passing on information to the Russians, people were heavily critical of the government for allowing two traitors to work so long in responsible positions without being detected.

The uproar was intensified when rumours began to circulate that Burgess and Maclean had been able to escape in time because they had been warned of their impending arrest by yet another traitor, this time one high in the ranks of the British secret service. At first the government denied the existence of this 'third man'. Later they announced that such a traitor had in fact existed. By this time it was too late for the 'third man', Kim Philby, a very senior member of the British intelligence services, had also defected to Russia.

Reeling from this series of disasters, the British counter-espionage services had some successes in unearthing traitors. In 1962, William Vassall, a clerk working in Naval Intelligence, was arrested and found guilty of photographing documents and passing them on to the Russians. He was sentenced to 18 years' imprisonment.

Vassall, who had served in Moscow for a time, had been blackmailed by the Russians, who had taken incriminating photographs of him at a drunken party. When it was discovered that the Russians were coming into possession of a great deal of secret information about British naval security arrangements, the leak was traced back to Vassall, who confessed at once.

Gordon Lonsdale and George Blake

Burgess, Maclean and Vassall were essentially amateur agents. Two spies operating in Great Britain who were much more professional in their approach were Gordon Lonsdale and George Blake.

When Gordon Lonsdale had left Colonel Abel in New York to operate a British spy network, he pretended to be a Canadian businessman. His real name was Konon Molody and he was born in Moscow. For a while he lived in the USA with an aunt, and there he learned excellent English. He returned to Russia shortly before the war.

Lonsdale fought with Russian guerrillas against the Germans, and after the war he served in Berlin, hunting down German war criminals. He was then sent to

53 Kim Philby seen talking to journalists at a press conference in 1955. Philby had probably been recruited by the Russians before the Second World War, but worked his way up to an extremely senior position in British Intelligence. He managed to warn Burgess and Maclean of their impending arrests before making his own escape. Today he lives and works in Russia

assist Abel in New York and subsequently went to Britain. It was his function in Britain to discover as much as he could about the country's submarine service. To assist him at the beginning he had two other professional agents, Peter Kroger and his wife Helen. The Krogers had bought a bungalow in Ruislip, a London suburb. The bungalow housed a radio transmitter capable of sending messages to Moscow. Ruislip had been selected as the location of the transmitter because of the presence close at hand of an American military airfield. Among all the radio messages passing to and from this airfield the Russians had correctly estimated that their own transmitter would pass undetected.

54 Ethel Gee seen returning home after her release from prison in 1970, having served her sentence for her part in the Portland Spy Ring case. She and her boy-friend Harry Houghton passed on secrets from the underwater research station at Portland to Gordon Lonsdale. Houghton spent the money he received too freely and aroused suspicion. He was put under observation, and led the authorities to the other spies

55 George Blake, seen here on the extreme left, with other former prisoners of the Chinese soon after their release from a North Korean internment camp in 1953. Blake was a prisoner in Korea for almost three years. After his return he began to work for the Communists with considerable success. He was caught and sentenced to a total of 42 years' imprisonment. He later escaped from prison

With his base and staff firmly established, Lonsdale looked for a method of penetrating the underwater weapons establishment at Portland. Here he was aided by his superiors in Moscow. They provided him with the name of a worker at Portland, Harry Houghton. Houghton had served at the British embassy at Warsaw and the Communists had noted him as a man likely to be susceptible to bribery.

Cautiously Lonsdale approached Houghton and offered him money to spy for Russia. Houghton agreed and he and his girl-friend, Ethel Gee, proceeded to pass on information to Lonsdale. Houghton proved careless in handling the money supplied by Lonsdale. The dockyard police at Portland noticed that he bought an expensive house and car and that he was spending more than he was supposed to be earning on drink alone.

This information was passed on to MI5. Houghton was watched and unwittingly led his shadowers to Lonsdale, who in turn took them to the Krogers. All the spies were arrested and sentenced to long terms of imprisonment at the beginning of 1961. In 1964 Lonsdale was exchanged for a British agent in Russian hands.

Lonsdale's prison sentence had been one of 25 years, but this was light compared with the 42 years which another agent, George Blake, received when he was found guilty of spying for the Communists.

As a young man, Blake, whose real name was Behar, escaped from German-occupied Holland at the beginning of the war and joined the intelligence branch of the British navy.

After the war, although not a British citizen, he was allowed to work for the Foreign Office. In 1950 he was sent to work in Korea and when war broke out he was captured by the North Koreans and imprisoned. It is not known whether Blake became a Communist during his captivity or whether he had joined the Communist party as a youth serving in the Dutch resistance. Certainly when the Korean war ended and Blake was released with other prisoners he was committed to spying for the Communists.

Naturally his superiors in the Foreign Office were ignorant of this and Blake was posted to Berlin as a member of MI6. Systematically he set out to wreck the British espionage organisation. He denied help to agents and was responsible for betraying dozens to the Russians. He also arranged the kidnapping of influential East Germans who had fled to the West.

Eventually Blake was betrayed by another double agent but not before he had practically crippled MI6 in Germany. He served only a few years of his prison sentence, escaping from a London gaol and disappearing.

Errors and embarrassments
The more successful an espionage exploit is, the less is known about it. Only the mistakes receive publicity; the successes are often not reported until years after the event, if at all.

It is therefore perhaps only natural that more is known about the failures of

56 (*Above*) Equipment found in the home of Oleg Lyalin—an example of the time and trouble spymasters devote to the technical apparatus issued to their agents. The hollowed-out torch batteries contain film. A pencil unscrews to reveal more film. There is a short-wave radio and a tape recorder. The documents include a code sheet and a radio signalling plan

57 (*Left*) This Russian spy kit was found in the possession of Douglas Britten, an RAF chief technician who was sentenced to 21 years' imprisonment for selling information to the Russians. The camera, which will operate in total darkness, was fitted inside the wallet. This is only one example of the technical ingenuity applied to espionage equipment

58 (*Below, left*) This miniature code book, easily concealed, was used for decoding messages from Moscow. Codes had been used by spies from the earliest times, but by the 1970s they were extremely complicated and hard to break down without access to a codebook

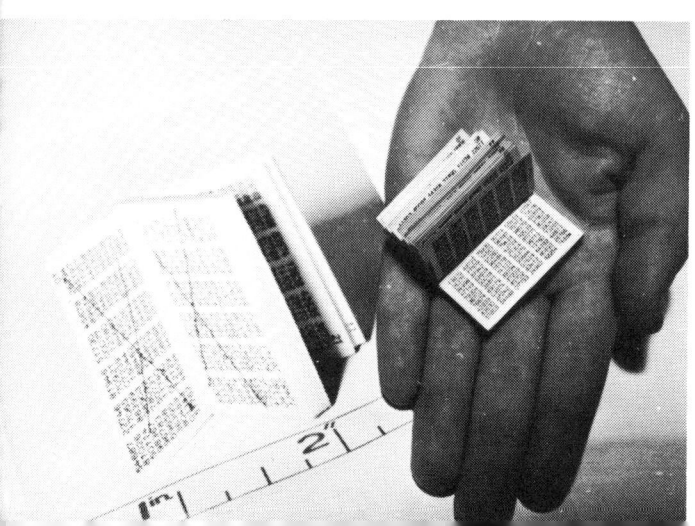

59 (*Right*) When the Ruislip bungalow of Russian agents Peter and Helen Kroger was searched, this radiogram was found. On examination it was found to conceal a tape recorder with headphones connected to it. This was only a small part of the equipment found in the Krogers' home

60 Secret messages are often concealed in microdots of the sort shown here. The message is written down and then compressed into the tiny microdots. The three microdots shown here have been enlarged approximately $1\frac{1}{2}$ times. On the right, one of the microdots has been enlarged to show the message. These were found in Helen Kroger's handbag when she was arrested with her husband Peter

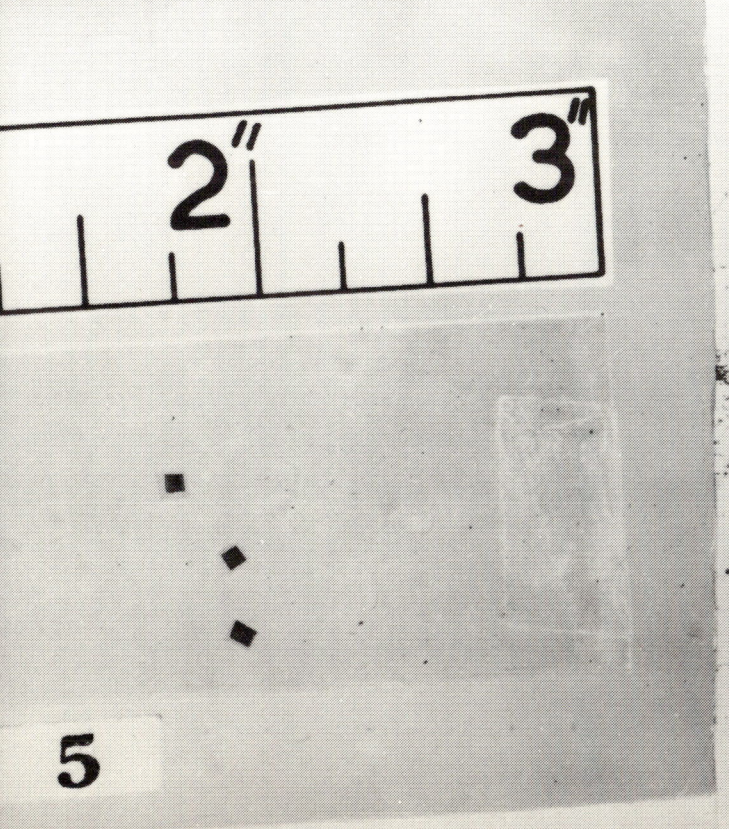

5

intelligence agencies than their achievements over the past few decades. Failures there have certainly been. In the United States, for example, great political embarrassment was caused to the Western powers when a U2 aircraft on a spying mission over Russia was forced down and the pilot, Gary Powers, arrested and brought to trial as a spy. Powers was sentenced to imprisonment and later was exchanged for Colonel Rudolf Abel, the imprisoned Russian spymaster.

An example of faulty intelligence occurred when the American Central Intelligence Agency advised President Kennedy that an invasion of Cuba from Miami by a group of exiled Cubans stood a good chance of overthrowing Communist President Castro. Kennedy allowed the invasion to take place and it was utterly crushed at the Bay of Pigs.

In Great Britain, too, similar misjudgements occurred. When a Russian warship anchored in Portsmouth harbour in 1956, a former frogman, Lionel 'Buster' Crabb, was sent out, almost certainly by a British intelligence unit, to swim around the cruiser and report on it. Crabb, neither young nor fully fit, never returned from his mission. Whether he had an accident or was captured or killed by the Russians was never known. Clumsy attempts to hush up the incident caused a storm of protest in Britain.

61 (*Left*) 'Buster' Crabb tells children about his search for a sunken treasure ship. His disappearance in 1956, probably while on a secret mission, was never explained

62 (*Right*) Superintendent Fred Cherrill was for many years the head of the Fingerprint Department at Scotland Yard. His expertise was responsible for convicting many criminals and spies. The Fingerprint Bureau was founded at Scotland Yard in 1901, but as early as 1857 Sir William Herschel of the Indian Civil Service had been using fingerprinting in Bengal to prevent Indians from impersonating each other in court

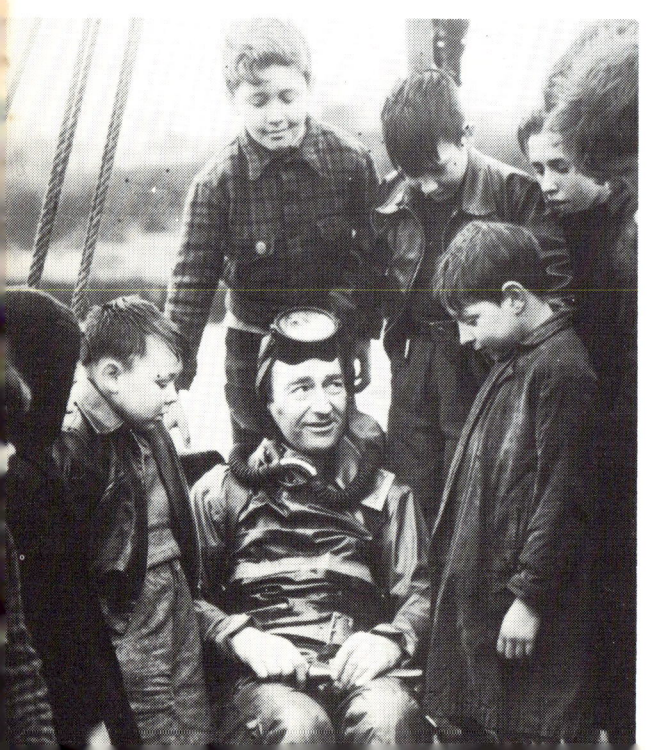

In 1963 there was further controversy when a government minister, John Profumo, resigned from his office because of a liason with a woman, Christine Keeler. It was discovered that among Christine Keeler's other associates was a Russian naval attaché, Eugene Ivanov, who was suspected of being an agent. There was no question of information being passed on, but many felt that British security organisations should have moved in more swiftly.

There was slightly better fortune in the case of Oleg Penkovsky, a senior Russian secret service official who defected to the West in 1961. However, Greville Wynn, a British businessman alleged to have helped arrange the defection, was arrested and imprisoned by the Russians. Later, he was exchanged for Gordon Lonsdale.

Industrial and political espionage

Espionage has never been confined to military spying operations. Industrial and political espionage have also attracted the dubious talents of men through the ages.

One of the first examples of industrial espionage in Europe involving an Englishman was that of Richard Foley, an ironmaster from the Midlands. In order to improve his own industrial techniques Foley would go on walking tours of Europe, attempting to discover the secrets of the ironmasters of Belgium, Germany, Italy and Spain. This seventeenth-century industrial agent had considerable success in his work.

Three hundred years later industrial espionage had become much more highly organised. Before the Second World War Japanese firms sent their young men all over the world to work in factories and laboratories with orders to observe and remember as much as possible. Upon their return to Japan the techniques discovered by the young men were put into practice in Japanese firms.

After the war industrial espionage became big business. One organisation claimed to specialise in obtaining secrets of processes and techniques for any firms able to afford such information. A number of court cases in the 1950s and 1960s revealed that industrial secrets were in great demand and that anyone able to provide secret information about manufacturing processes could usually be sure of a good price for it. One court case in America was brought because a scientist working for one firm wished to leave and work in the laboratories of another firm. It was claimed that the scientist knew so many secret processes that it would give his new firm an unfair advantage over the one he had previously worked for! The scientist was allowed to join the other firm, but he was solemnly warned that he must not use in his new work any information he had discovered in his previous job.

Security firms proliferated in the post-war years in an effort to guard industrial secrets. At the same time the latest technological developments were adapted for use in dock and airport security arrangements.

An odd off-shoot of industrial espionage was the growth of so-called 'head-hunting' firms. These were organisations which, for a price, would fill the top executive posts in companies. In order to discover details about the backgrounds of executives likely to be of use to them some of these firms developed massive security files about top workers.

There were also examples of espionage among British trade unions. This was particularly true of the Electrical Trades Union. During the war control of this Union had fallen into Communist hands, largely due to the apathy of the majority of its members. In the 1950s and 1960s there was a bitter struggle for the leadership of the Union. In an effort to retain control the Communists, it was alleged, resorted to various espionage practices, forging of ballots and other illegal activities. The Union was expelled from both the Trades Union Congress and the Labour Party. It was readmitted in 1962, by which time the malpractices had ceased.

A notorious example of political espionage occurred in 1972 when certain Republicans were accused of planting listening devices in the offices of the Democratic Party headquarters at the Watergate building in the USA. By means of these bugging devices outsiders could listen to conversations being held in the Democratic headquarters. Many senior officials in the American government were implicated and President Nixon appeared on television to deny publicly that he was involved in the conspiracy or subsequent attempts to conceal it. It was revealed however that the White House itself was bugged so that the President had records of all conversations that took place in his office.

Espionage in fiction

Spying has been a favourite theme for writers of fiction for many years. The first twentieth-century spy novel to achieve large sales was written in 1903. This was the *Riddle of the Sands* by Erskine Childers, a thrilling story set off the east coast of England. The author himself was to have a most adventurous life, serving in the Boer War and winning the DSO for gallantry in the Royal Navy in the First World War. He was arrested for assisting the Sinn Fein in the struggle for Irish independence and executed in 1922.

Many other writers followed Childers and some of the later Victorian authors in writing tales of espionage. One of the most famous was John Buchan, whose

63 This British woman was a double agent in Australia. She pretended to be working for a Russian spy ring while all the time passing information on to the Australian authorities. As a result of her activities, the spy ring was smashed, and a high Soviet official of the Canberra embassy was expelled from Australia. The documents and photographs being examined were used as evidence against the spies

64 Reporters seen watching President Nixon on television talking about the Watergate Scandal. The publicity given to the matter by newspapers and television led to a public investigation of the 'bugging' of the Democratic Party Headquarters at the Watergate Building in Washington. It was later revealed that the White House itself was bugged so that the President had a record of all his conversations there

masterpiece was probably *The 39 Steps*, an outstanding 'chase' thriller. Buchan used one character, the agent Richard Hannay, for many of his books, and this use of a central character in successive novels was adopted by a number of writers, particularly the one who used the name 'Sapper' and wrote the *Bulldog Drummond* series.

After the Second World War, spy thrillers became more popular than ever. Eventually, however, it seemed that most novels of espionage could be divided into one of two main categories. They were either understated, grimly realistic books of the type written before the war by Graham Greene (*The Confidential Agent*, etc) and later by John Le Carre (*The Spy Who Came in from the Cold*); or they were flamboyant, tongue-in-cheek stories featuring almost indestructible heroes and grotesque villains. Perhaps the best examples of the latter were the James Bond books written by Ian Fleming, which also became very popular and successful films. Television, too, saw the introduction of many espionage features and plays.

Further Reading——
Murphey and Alexander, *The Global Age* (Hart Davis).
Pelling, *A History of British Trade Unionism* (Pelican).
Reid, *Tongues of Conscience* (Constable).

Index

The numbers in **bold type** refer to pages on which illustrations appear.